College Faculty: Versatile Human Resources in a Period of Constraint

Roger G. Baldwin, Robert T. Blackburn, *Editors*

NEW DIRECTIONS FOR INSTITUTIONAL RESEARCH

Sponsored by the Association for Institutional Research

MARVIN W. PETERSON, *Editor-in-Chief*
PATRICK T. TERENZINI, *Associate Editor*

Number 40, December 1983

Paperback sourcebooks in
The Jossey-Bass Higher Education Series

Jossey-Bass Inc., Publishers
San Francisco • Washington • London

Roger G. Baldwin, Robert T. Blackburn (Eds.).
College Faculty: Versatile Human Resources in a Period of Constraint.
New Directions for Institutional Research, no. 40.
Volume X, number 4.
San Francisco: Jossey-Bass, 1983

New Directions for Institutional Research Series
Marvin W. Peterson, *Editor-in-Chief,* Patrick T. Terenzini, *Associate Editor*

New Directions for Institutional Research (publication number
USPS 098-830) is published quarterly by Jossey-Bass Inc.,
Publishers, and is sponsored by the Association for Institutional
Research. The volume and issue numbers above are included for
the convenience of libraries. Second-class postage rates paid at
San Francisco, California, and at additional mailing offices.

Correspondence:
Subscriptions, single-issue orders, change of address notices,
undelivered copies, and other correspondence should be sent to
New Directions Subscriptions, Jossey-Bass Inc., Publishers,
433 California Street, San Francisco, California 94104.

Editorial correspondence should be sent to the Editor-in-Chief,
Marvin W. Peterson, Center for the Study of Higher Education,
University of Michigan, Ann Arbor, Michigan 48109, or
Patrick T. Terenzini, Office of Institutional Research, SUNY,
Albany, New York 12222.

Library of Congress Catalogue Card Number LC 82-84193

International Standard Serial Number ISSN 0271-0579

International Standard Book Number ISBN 87589-958-7

Cover art by Willi Baum
Manufactured in the United States of America

Ordering Information

The paperback sourcebooks listed below are published quarterly and can be ordered either by subscription or single-copy.

Subscriptions cost $35.00 per year for institutions, agencies, and libraries. Individuals can subscribe at the special rate of $21.00 per year *if payment is by personal check.* (Note that the full rate of $35.00 applies if payment is by institutional check, even if the subscription is designated for an individual.) Standing orders are accepted. Subscriptions normally begin with the first of the four sourcebooks in the current publication year of the series. When ordering, please indicate if you prefer your subscription to begin with the first issue of the *coming* year.

Single copies are available at $7.95 when payment accompanies order, and *all single-copy orders under $25.00 must include payment.* (California, New Jersey, New York, and Washington, D.C., residents please include appropriate sales tax.) For billed orders, cost per copy is $7.95 plus postage and handling. (Prices subject to change without notice.)

Bulk orders (ten or more copies) of any individual sourcebook are available at the following discounted prices: 10–49 copies, $7.15 each; 50–100 copies, $6.35 each; over 100 copies, *inquire.* Sales tax and postage and handling charges apply as for single copy orders.

To ensure correct and prompt delivery, all orders must give either the *name of an individual* or an *official purchase order number.* Please submit your order as follows:

Subscriptions: specify series and year subscription is to begin.
Single Copies: specify sourcebook code (such as, IR8) and first two words of title.

Mail orders for United States and Possessions, Latin America, Canada, Japan, Australia, and New Zealand to:
Jossey-Bass Inc., Publishers
433 California Street
San Francisco, California 94104

Mail orders for all other parts of the world to:
Jossey-Bass Limited
28 Banner Street
London EC1Y 8QE

New Directions for Institutional Research Series

Marvin W. Peterson, *Editor-in-Chief*
Patrick T. Terenzini, *Associate Editor*

Contents

Editors' Notes

The well-being of the academic profession is a subject of growing concern throughout the higher education community. In recent years many reports and articles have expressed this concern, particularly for the career prospects of professors in less popular academic fields or in unstable academic insitutions. Anxiety has grown for the welfare of higher education in general as opportunities to hire young professors and enlarge faculties have decreased significantly. It seems clear that if colleges and universities are to prosper in the next two decades, they must reevaluate human resource needs and reassess personnel policies and practices. Higher education institutions must discover new ways to utilize current human resources, especially faculty members, more creatively and productively. This sourcebook considers how attention to faculty resources can help to preserve educational vitality in a period of fiscal constraint.

In Chapter One, Blackburn and Baldwin discuss why human resource development can benefit colleges and universities. The authors, however, make it clear that human resource issues are complex. They suggest that it is necessary to examine personal, professional, and environmental variables that affect professors in order for institutions to accurately assess the current needs of faculty.

Chapter Two reviews some of the best sources of data on the condition of the professoriate and discusses what important dimensions of the faculty status question remain unexamined. Baldwin and Blackburn suggest what types of local information on faculty members institutions should collect to supplement aggregate national data. The authors conclude that the information needed to understand faculty conditions differs by type of institution and academic field, among other variables.

In Chapter Three, Lee considers the question of future demand for college professors at both national and institutional levels. She contends that the national data on faculty staffing trends are woefully inadequate. She recommends, therefore, that a combination of national and local data is necessary in order to project a college or university's future staffing needs. Lee suggests that an enriched data base outlining professors' skills, interests, and areas of expertise would enable colleges to utilize the full range of their professors' talents more effectively.

Early retirement and career change incentives represent

1

another means to preserve flexibility in the academic work force. In Chapter Four, Patton outlines the basic attributes of such programs but warns that career transition incentives, to be effective, must accommodate institutional staffing needs and complement other personnel practices.

Next, McKeachie employs the literature on aging to consider effective ways to renew faculty members. He concludes that, although individuals differ greatly, persons of all ages have the ability to change. The task for higher education institutions is to create an environment that supports, rather than inhibits, professional growth.

Nelsen, in Chapter Six, continues the discussion of strategies to renew faculty resources. He reviews common faculty development needs and considers what faculty development practices seem to have the greatest positive impact.

Then, in a publication that champions the importance of human resource development, Toombs plays the thought provoking role of devil's advocate. He sounds a note of caution by questioning the long-term effects of current efforts to rejuvenate college faculty. Toombs asserts that most of academe's personnel policies were designed to retain professors in a period of scarce faculty resources. In this era of abundant faculty talent, however, Toombs believes personnel procedures that encourage a "dynamic flow of ability" through institutions will best preserve educational vitality. His chapter presents examples of policies that could enhance flexibility in faculty staffing.

The final chapter comments on many of the profound and complex human resource issues raised in the preceding chapters. The editors rely on historical precedent to state an optimistic prognosis for the future. Although colleges and universities confront a complex assortment of faculty staffing problems, Blackburn and Baldwin cite difficult periods earlier in this century that the academic profession has survived. They are confident that the profession will also withstand the current challenge since problem solving is a fundamental objective of higher education.

Roger G. Baldwin
Robert T. Blackburn
Editors

Roger G. Baldwin is assistant to the provost at Wittenberg University. From 1980 to 1982, he was research associate at the American Association for Higher Education, where he conducted a nationwide study of college and university programs designed to expand professors' career options.

Robert T. Blackburn is professor of higher education in the Center for the Study of Higher Education at the University of Michigan. His research focus is the academic career.

In a labor-intensive enterprise like higher education,
human resources are the most valuable commodity.

Faculty as Human Resources: Reality and Potential

Robert T. Blackburn
Roger G. Baldwin

Nearly a decade ago, Bailey (1974, p. 27) wrote that "the most important thing about a college is the quality of the lives of the people who staff it." This statement is probably more accurate today than it was then. In a labor-intensive enterprise like higher education, human resources are the most valuable commodity. The vitality and effectiveness of a college or university is directly linked to the quality, resourcefulness, and vigor of its faculty members.

However, staffing a higher education institution is not simply a matter of filling positions with "people who presently are capable of doing them competently" (Porter and others, 1975, p. 189). Colleges and universities exist in a rapidly changing environment. The human resource skills needed to operate a college evolve over time. Hence, it is necessary for institutions to monitor their productivity and human resource needs on an ongoing basis in order to assure that they derive maximum benefit from their faculty members.

Human resources require careful study and planning, just as economic and physical resources do. No responsible academic institution would commit funds to a new library or theater complex without

R. G. Baldwin and R. T. Blackburn (Eds.). *College Faculty: Versatile Human Resources in a Period of Constraint.*
New Directions for Institutional Research, no. 40. San Francisco: Jossey-Bass, December 1983.

assurances that the facilities would meet important educational needs. Likewise, responsible institutions should not invest large sums in faculty salaries and support services without keeping track of the return on their investment. Colleges and universities can no longer afford to take their human resources for granted. To preserve quality in the 1980s and 1990s, effective use of faculty resources is vital.

New Shape of an Ongoing Human Resource Problem

Concern for the effective use of faculty resources is not a new issue in higher education. To quote the Carnegie Commission on Higher Education (1972, p. 26), "What is different is the problem's current shape and intensity." A combination of negative circumstances makes it difficult for higher education institutions to keep pace with emerging educational needs. Overburdened financial resources limit professors' opportunities to conduct research or to travel and participate in professional development activities. Funds for supplies and support services have declined at almost all institutions. Opportunities for "psychic relief" (Bailey, 1974, p. 24) from the routine of the academic career have diminished substantially and threaten the morale of those in the academic profession.

Long-term prospects for advancement in the academic career are also discouraging for many faculty members. Low retirement rates and steady-state conditions in higher education have virtually eliminated career mobility for many college professors. Few have the opportunity to move on to challenging new assignments either where they currently work or at some other college or university. Moreover, limited faculty hiring is gradually increasing the mean age of the professoriate and the generation gap that inevitably develops between students and professors. Many academic institutions are losing the "ginger of newness" (Bailey, 1974, p. 24) once provided by a steady influx of fresh, enthusiastic new professors.

During the next two decades, this combination of unfavorable circumstances will undoubtedly have a significant impact on individual faculty members and on the institutions in which they work. It limits institutions' ability to add new courses and to introduce new subject fields. With too many faculty at the wrong age (mid career, far from retirement) or in the wrong fields (that is, ones with declining enrollment), colleges find it difficult to respond to shifting enrollment patterns or expanding areas of knowledge. Due to these same unfavorable circumstances, the future of most professors is tied much more intimately than it was in the past to the fate of their present institution (Carnegie Council on Policy Studies in Higher Education, 1980).

Higher education institutions that desire to prosper in the years ahead must find ways of adapting their programs in spite of severe limits on their resources. Already, colleges and universities have taken a wide range of actions to maintain their responsiveness to changing educational circumstances. Faculty development programs, increased hiring of part-time instructors, tenure quotas, and early retirement policies all represent efforts to maintain flexible, productive faculty resources. As yet, special program and policy adjustments of this sort have not been sufficient to preserve educational vitality. In the lean years ahead, academic institutions must use all their resources— including their human resources—more flexibly and more creatively if they wish to ensure long-term survival.

Toward Effective Use of Faculty Resources

One of the principal managerial problems of a higher education organization is to match institutional resources with student demand. Some disjuncture between student interests and faculty resources is inevitable (Stadtman, 1980). Of course, the problem becomes more complex in a period when there is little opportunity to hire new teaching staff. For example, Carnegie Council data indicate that enrollment in professional majors increased from 38 percent in 1969 to 58 percent in 1977. During the same period, enrollment in the humanities dropped from 9 percent to 5 percent and physical science enrollments declined from 7 percent to 4 percent. However, faculty positions in these teaching fields changed hardly at all during this period, and the result was some serious imbalances in the distribution of faculty resources (Stadtman, 1980).

Pondering higher education's resource problems, Bailey (1974, p. 26) asked: "Is there a chance that the traumas of diminishing resources. . . can be mitigated by attention to qualitative changes in the lives of all those associated with institutions of higher education?. . . Can we help those who remain to start growing again?" Colleges and universities should answer Bailey's question with a confident yes. Efficient use of faculty resources can open a wide array of professional growth opportunities that can help to maintain an institution's vitality and effectiveness. However, the human resource questions facing higher education are not simple. Colleges and universities must consider how they can derive maximum benefit from their precious faculty resources, how they can create a climate that will stimulate faculty growth and adaptation, and how they can promote professors' self-actualization.

Higher education typically has not been farsighted with regard to its human resources. Student interests and faculty needs frequently become known only after the fact. Consequently, it often takes several years before institutions can reallocate their resources to provide the courses that students desire or the services that faculty need (Stadtman, 1980). However, to be successful in today's volatile environment, higher education institutions and the faculty whom they employ must anticipate and adapt to one another's needs. Professors must be able to adjust their skills to changing educational demands, or their colleges will lose their ability to compete for students. Similarly, institutional objectives must accommodate the career goals of the people whom they wish to develop, or professors' morale will inevitably suffer. A convergence of individuals' career goals and the organization's development plans can promote growth beneficial at both the individual and the institutional level (Porter and others, 1975).

One of the most effective ways of changing an organization is to change the people who comprise it. Colleges that wish to adapt to the educational objectives of the 1980s should capitalize on the natural flexibility and growth potential of their human resources. By influencing the attitudes, skills, and behavior of faculty members, higher education institutions can revise their programs, expand their services, and generally enhance their effectiveness (Porter and others, 1975).

Unfortunately, colleges and universities typically do not take advantage of the full range of skills that their faculty members possess. They tend to fit professors into narrow classifications defined by disciplinary specialities and overlook a diverse array of other talents and interests that professors bring. As a rule, academics are broadly educated people. Often, their principal teaching field represents only a portion of their store of knowledge and experience. By viewing faculty as general institutional resources, not solely as information specialists, higher education institutions can capitalize on professors' latent talents.

Tannenbaum and Davis (1969, p. 71) describe "the tremendous untapped potential in most individuals [that is] yearning for discovery and release." Proponents of organizational development adhere to two main value assumptions that derive from a strong belief in human potential. They assert, first, that individuals have an inherent capacity for growth and, second, that individuals also have a desire for growth (Porter and others, 1975). College professors possess these attributes in abundance. They have demonstrated that they are intelligent. They are motivated, and they have considerable self-discipline. Above all, they are good learners. The key human resource goal for a higher education institution is to promote professors' self-actualization by facilitating their natural growth and by bringing about more complete utilization of the total person.

One major way in which colleges can adapt to changing educational needs and still meet budgetary constraints is by improving their use of faculty. However, human resources are more difficult to manipulate than economic or physical assets. They can be difficult to develop and maintain. Human resources are perishable. If they are not employed properly, they can atrophy and become ineffective. Hence, higher education institutions must give special consideration to their faculty members if they are to achieve maximum benefit from them. They must be sensitive to professors' interests, aspirations, and the overall quality of their work life. The ability of organizations to develop their staff members effectively is directly related to the degree to which institutional objectives coincide with the objectives of the people whom they wish to develop (Porter and others, 1975). Thus, colleges and universities must try to maintain conditions that favor professional growth at the same time that they try to adapt educational programs to shifting student demands. Institutions must maintain an ongoing dialogue with their faculty members to ensure that faculty understand their circumstances, needs, and objectives and vice versa. In this way, institutional and individual actions can complement one another and work toward common goals.

Collecting Relevant Information

Colleges can stimulate the development of their faculty resources by gathering and sharing data on many variables that are directly relevant to professors' careers. Information on enrollment trends, tenure ratios, financial conditions, funding opportunities, and training programs can sensitize faculty members to institutional needs and to their own professional growth options. By maintaining up-to-date information on faculty and institutional conditions, colleges can help faculty members to plan their career path in line with their own development goals. A well-stocked human resource data bank can enable colleges and universities to anticipate emerging trends within their faculty. By monitoring faculty satisfaction, work load, age distribution, and other important variables, higher education institutions can adapt their policies and redesign positions to capitalize effectively on new or underutilized capabilities within the ranks of their faculty. Awareness of changing institutional conditions and faculty attributes enables colleges and universities to offer challenging assignments and novel growth opportunities that maintain enthusiasm among professors who must respond to changing educational circumstances (Porter and others, 1975).

Of course, it is easy to advocate that colleges and universities should be sensitive to conditions that influence the effectiveness of their faculty members. It is less easy, however, to determine the specific factors that institutions should monitor in order to assess the human resource climate on their campus accurately. Information needs vary from campus to campus. Data that are useful at one college can be less relevant at another. Essentially, each institution needs periodically to take the pulse of its faculty resources. It should examine the personal and professional attributes of its faculty members and the environmental characteristics that influence their performance. In order to utilize faculty resources effectively, higher education institutions must assess professors' circumstances and needs from a variety of relevant perspectives.

Professors' Personal and Professional Attributes

First, colleges and universities should monitor the personal and professional variables related to professors' performance. We know that faculty feed more on internal rewards than they do on external ones (McKeachie, 1979). It is not that money is unimportant to faculty—its deficiency causes dissatisfaction—but rather that academics make primary decisions about what college to join and what activities to perform more on the basis of the conditions of work than they do on the dollars and cents that are offered. Stimulating and competent colleagues and students, the opportunity to teach courses that one desires, opportunities for scholarly growth—these are what give faculty their major satisfactions and rewards. Hence, we need to keep track of the level of professors' satisfaction and the factors that foster or inhibit such satisfaction.

Second, most of what we know about faculty careers comes from studies of male academics or from a mix of the sexes, with males in the majority. When the sexes are compared, differences in such matters as role preference (teaching over research, for example) and scholarly publications frequently appear. However, many of the results are debatable and certainly depend on factors other than sex. For example, for females, marital status leads to different predictions. Publication rates for never-married females differ very little from rates for males. Married or not currently married differ. Nothing is known about homosexuals of either sex. In any event, the institution that is concerned about the well-being of faculty should carefully examine the career circumstances of all types of professors.

Third, while tenure is once again under attack and some colleges and universities are trying alternative models, the evidence does not support the repeated assertion that tenure is the cause of faculty unwillingness to change, illiberalism, decreased or discontinued scholarly output, or dull teaching. Faculty who are tenured are not different on most dimensions from faculty who are not (Blackburn, 1972).

Fourth, career stage seems to matter (Baldwin and Blackburn, 1981; Blackburn and Havighurst, 1979). Interests, desires, worries, and the like fluctuate over time and need to be considered by the sensitive institution. Furthermore, the critical career events for individual faculty also depend on the individual's vocational emphasis — teaching, research, or service. (Longitudinal studies are few in number, and the information just cited needs to be taken with caution.) Therefore, it is imperative for colleges and universities to recognize important developmental differences among professors.

Fifth, institutions should be sensitive to the differences that exist among faculty subcultures. These differences can be identified with traditional disciplines and professional schools. Values and norms vary appreciably across units. Business expects its faculty to consult and would consider individuals who do not as lacking, whereas many arts and science departments judge a colleague who consults with some regularity as not a true academic. Other differences across departments and schools include basic intellectual paradigms, concern for faculty governance and administrative structures, ways of dealing with students, and teaching modes. In addition, there is also variation within the subgroups. Efforts to maintain faculty vitality need to take matters related to academic specialty into consideration.

Last, there are additional psychological attributes that are probably related to faculty vitality. Unfortunately, research in this domain is limited. No large-scale studies have included basic psychological traits of faculty. When data have been collected on such characteristics as flexibility, self-esteem, and anxiety, they have been shown to interrelate with stress and performance on the job (for example, student judgments of teaching effectiveness) (Clark and Blackburn, 1973). Higher education institutions should be cognizant of the ways in which important psychological traits interact with professors' work. By monitoring relevant personal and professional attributes of faculty members, colleges and universities can develop policies and services that meet professors' needs and facilitate their ongoing development.

Environmental Characteristics

Environmental characteristics related to faculty performance also require careful observation. The environment in which faculty work can be conceptualized by its structural components and by its interpersonal aspects. These aspects can then be divided between those which are formally arranged and designed and those which occur on an informal ad hoc basis. This fourfold division can be used to identify and improve the environmental conditions that affect faculty vitality.

Formal/Structural. Libraries, laboratories, and similar essential facilities necessary for faculty to conduct their work all fall into the formal/structural category. Moreover, formal human arrangements are just as important as bricks and mortar in supporting faculty vitality. Networks through the committee structure and task forces are two examples of such arrangements. So, too, is administrative leadership when it exposes faculty to new issues and problems to be solved and when it develops an esprit that energizes individual and group efforts to attain excellence and to meet higher standards of accomplishment and performance.

As obvious as such formal structures are, external forces can erode them all too easily if their need is not kept constantly in mind. When dollars are short, the temptation for administrators to increase faculty work load, to trim the library budget by not matching increases with rising costs, and to spend their time not on academic leadership but on budget matters is almost irresistible. The danger in such actions is that the resulting small savings will be more than offset by decreased faculty vitality. To prevent negative conditions from developing, it is important to monitor how conditions within the formal/structural environment affect professors.

Formal/Personal. Classes, symposia, lecture and concert series, and other regularly scheduled formal structures bring members of the community of faculty and students together and provide opportunities for faculty growth. Each of these structures is a potential source of new ideas and stimulation, although they are not always used with this goal in mind. For example, charging a group of faculty to redesign the college's general education program—say by the creation of interdisciplinary courses—provides an excellent opportunity for colleagues to learn from one another. A new literature is explored, other modes of teaching are identified, and novel solutions to problems are entertained.

Such activities as these and others like them—faculty explorations with business and industry, temporary assignments on institutional projects, or off-campus classes in nontraditional settings—that encourage faculty to exchange ideas and take on new challenges can be systematically built into the ongoing life of colleges and universities. By studying the formal/personal environment on campus, institutions can better facilitate the kind of faculty growth and development that they desire to promote.

Informal/Structural. Professional meetings, journals, information networks, and other forms of systematic exchange are a part of the regular structure of higher education. They provide the stimulus as well as the knowledge necessary for further growth and activity. One of the strongest predictors of productive people is the frequency and number of persons with whom they maintain semiformal contact.

Here, too, the implications are obvious. At the same time, however, some of the actions taken run counter to the intended goals. Economic efficiency is often translated into reducing the telephone bill, especially for long-distance calls. Reducing conference attendance is defended on the grounds that the papers presented can be obtained by mail. Yet, it is not the papers themselves that contribute new ideas to faculty but the informal exchanges in corridors and restaurants. The cost of reducing this kind of faculty activity can be high. To maintain a healthy professional climate, colleges and universities should periodically examine their informal/structural environment and assess how well it supports faculty vitality.

Informal/Personal. The informal/personal includes all the special kinds of relationships between individuals that make a difference in career development and continued growth. The role of senior professor with a novitiate, the sponsor or mentor with her or his protege, and the friendships that both support and challenge colleagues are not formally built into college and university structures and probably cannot be. Still, there are ways in which institutional leaders can increase the likelihood that such relationships will develop. Senior faculty enjoy the mentoring role. This type of liaison would occur more frequently if administrative leadership created conditions that encouraged collaboration among novice and veteran faculty. Seed money for grant development that stipulated senior-junior pairing is one easy way of encouraging productive faculty interaction. So are committee appointments and office arrangements that bring faculty into close contact with one another. Information on the informal/personal climate of an institution can help colleges and universities to determine how they can foster creative and stimulating alliances among professors.

Conclusion

The proper combination of personal and professional variables with supportive environmental conditions needs to be established on a campus in order to capitalize fully on valuable faculty resources. Person-environment fit theory (French and others, 1982) helps to illustrate the important relationship that exists between individuals and their work

14

environment. Information on significant faculty attributes and environmental factors that are related to professors' performance can clarify the person-environment fit at an institution. Hence, such information can suggest the kinds of actions that colleges and universities should take in order to foster faculty vitality.

References

Bailey, S. K. "The Effective Use of Human Resources." In *The Effective Use of Resources: Financial and Human.* Washington, D.C.: Association of Governing Boards, 1974.

Baldwin, R. G., and Blackburn, R. T. "The Academic Career as a Developmental Process: Implications for Higher Education." *Journal of Higher Education,* 1981, *52* (6), 598–614.

Blackburn, R. T. *Tenure: Aspects of Job Security on the Changing Campus.* Research Monograph No. 19. Atlanta: Southern Regional Education Board, 1972.

Blackburn, R. T., and Havighurst, R. J. "Career Patterns of Distinguished Male Social Scientists." *Higher Education,* 1979, *8,* 553–572.

Carnegie Commission on Higher Education. *The More Effective Use of Resources: An Imperative for Higher Education.* New York: McGraw-Hill, 1972.

Carnegie Council on Policy Studies in Higher Education. *Three Thousand Futures: The Next Twenty Years for Higher Education.* San Francisco: Jossey-Bass, 1980.

Clark, M. J., and Blackburn, R. T. "Faculty Performance Under Stress." In A. L. Sockloff (Ed.), *Faculty Effectiveness as Evaluated by Students.* Philadelphia: Temple University, 1973.

French, J. R. P., Jr., Caplan, R. D., and Harrison, R. V. *The Mechanisms of Job Stress and Strain.* New York: Wiley, 1982.

McKeachie, W. J. "Perspectives from Psychology: Financial Incentives Are Ineffective for Faculty." In D. R. Lewis and W. E. Becker, Jr. (Eds.), *Academic Rewards in Higher Education.* Cambridge, Mass.: Ballinger, 1979.

Porter, L. W., and others. *Behavior in Organizations.* New York: McGraw-Hill, 1975.

Stadtman, V. A. *Academic Adaptations: Higher Education Prepares for the 1980s and 1990s.* San Francisco: Jossey-Bass, 1980.

Tannenbaum, R., and Davis, S. A. "Values, Man, and Organizations." *Industrial Management Review,* 1969, *10* (2), 67–86.

Robert T. Blackburn is professor of higher education in the Center for the Study of Higher Education at the University of Michigan.

Roger G. Baldwin is assistant to the provost at Wittenberg University.

Attention to the condition of the professoriate can help higher education institutions to employ their human resources more effectively.

The Condition of the Professoriate: The Variables and the Data Bases

Roger G. Baldwin
Robert T. Blackburn

The condition of the professoriate is directly related to the health and vigor of colleges and universities. As Smith (1978, p. 1) writes, "A university is its faculty. The excellence of a university is the excellence of its faculty." A higher education institution cannot prosper for long if its professors are overworked, underpaid, or out of touch with their discipline or their students.

Many factors currently threaten the well-being of American academics. Declining enrollments, limited opportunities for career advancement, and salaries that fail to keep pace with inflation are only a few of the negative conditions that confront professors today. In order to help faculty members cope with such a difficult environment, institutions must keep track of the conditions that affect the quality of faculty members' professional lives. By assessing the condition of the professoriate, colleges and universities can initiate the steps needed to maintain the vitality and effectiveness of their most valuable human resource.

R. G. Baldwin and R. T. Blackburn (Eds.). *College Faculty: Versatile Human Resources in a Period of Constraint.*
New Directions for Institutional Research, no. 40. San Francisco: Jossey-Bass, December 1983.

Assessing the Condition of the Professoriate

In order to measure the current state of members of the academic profession accurately, it is necessary to examine them from a broad perspective. Too frequently, the overall condition of college teachers is equated with their economic well-being. Buying power is certainly an important variable, but it is only part of the picture. Any effort to assess the condition of the professoriate should examine the economic, professional, and personal factors that affect the performance of college and university professors.

Economic Factors. Salary and fringe benefits are the principal economic indicators of faculty well-being. Data on the income of professors are essential to assess their overall state of affairs. Such information permits us to determine how faculty are faring in relation to trends in the national economy and in comparison to professionals in other fields. If we learn that professors' salaries have fallen behind those of peers elsewhere, we can assume that faculty morale will suffer.

Professional Variables. A number of professional variables must also be monitored if we are to understand the condition of the academic profession. These variables include workload, productivity, strengths and weaknesses, tenure ratios, age and rank distribution, mobility, and working conditions. A professor's workload can tell us much about the quality of his or her professional life. Information on the number of hours worked per week and the distribution of time among teaching, research, and service, consulting, and other employment can help to clarify the faculty condition. Data on the proportion of college teachers working full-time and part-time can also indicate how the institution divides its commitments and energy.

Data on faculty performance and professional contributions provide a direct measure of professors' effectiveness. Evaluations by students and colleagues, records of grants sought and received and publications produced, and information on professors' involvement in the life of their institution all serve as indications of the level of faculty vigor and achievement.

The skills and expertise to function as a professor are in a continuous process of evolution. For this reason, it is important to keep track of changing faculty strengths and areas of weakness. For example, we know that computer literacy will soon be necessary if one is to work effectively as a professional, but do we know what percentage of the professoriate is computer literate? Information on professors' talents and skills can uncover professional areas that deserve to be developed as well as unique strengths that can be utilized more effectively.

Data on the tenure status of professors are needed to estimate the faculty's flexibility, openness to new assignments, and ability to respond to changing educational circumstances.

Professors' motivations, problems, and satisfactions frequently vary from one career stage to another. An accurate assessment of faculty attributes requires information on the distribution of faculty by age and rank.

It is generally agreed that a moderate degree of faculty mobility among colleges and universities is beneficial to higher education. Knowledge of faculty mobililty patterns can help to identify the professors who are unsettled academic nomads, those who are productive, vital scholars, and those who have lost their professional momentum. Data on mobility can also indicate the segments of the academic community that need special professional development support in order to protect their career vitality.

Finally, faculty members' well-being is also a function of work environment. Hence, professors' assessment of the adequacy of instructional facilities, research equipment, and faculty support services is another reflection of the quality of their work lives.

Personal Variables. Information on personal variables, such as professors' objectives and attitudes, is also needed to describe the state of the academic profession. At least three variables—career objectives, career satisfaction, and stress—need to be examined.

A vital faculty should have both concrete short-term goals and long-term aspirations. By identifying professors' objectives, it becomes possible to estimate their level of motivation, their career development needs, and their prospects for future career success.

Information on how well professors like their teaching position or the institution in which they work can point to critical problems that need to be remedied. Career satisfaction is related to the quality of professors' performance. Hence, this variable also needs to be monitored.

Finally, data on faculty stress can be the most important indicator of the professoriate's condition. While a certain amount of career anxiety may be healthy, colleges and universities should know when stress levels become debilitating.

Sources of Data

Accurate assessment of the condition of members of the academic profession requires information from many different sources. Some national and state data on faculty are distributed annually. Some other useful data are readily available, but they are updated on a less regular basis. Finally, some information needed to understand the state of faculty requires local research tailored to the circumstances of a particular educational system, institution, or disciplinary field. To stay abreast of important trends, one should be familiar with the major sources of data on the American professorite.

Data on Economic Factors. Information on the economic status of college faculty is collected annually and disseminated by numerous organizations. Data on faculty compensation—both salary and fringe benefits—by rank, sex, discipline, type of institution, region of the country, and other related variables are available to clarify the circumstances of various subgroups of the professoriate.

Each year the American Association of University Professors (AAUP) publishes an annual report on the economic status of the profession in *Academe.* This report provides data on trends in salaries and benefits for faculty in general and for various faculty subgroups based on discipline, sex, tenure status, and academic rank. The AAUP report relates trends in faculty compensation to the Consumer Price Index and to the income of other professional groups. The report provides average salary data for more than 2,500 colleges and universities in the United States and classifies salary levels by institutional type.

Each year, the *Chronicle of Higher Education* publishes AAUP's data on faculty compensation by institution. Throughout the year, it also presents reports on a variety of economic issues directly relevant to professors. For example, the *Chronicle* regularly tracks academic salaries in comparison to the cost of living. It also monitors such topics as outside income earned by professors, salary trends in particular academic fields, and faculty income data by sex. Because of its wide coverage, the *Chronicle of Higher Education* can serve as a barometer of emerging developments in colleges and universities. Its reports on faculty compensation are likely to represent issues of concern to large segments of the professoriate.

The National Center for Education Statistics (NCES) annually publishes a *Digest of Education Statistics* and *The Condition of Education* which update salary data on professors in various types of colleges and universities.

The *Fact Book for Academic Administrators,* published annually by the American Council on Education, assembles a variety of useful information on faculty salaries and overall compensation. It provides average faculty salaries by academic rank and type of institution. The *Fact Book*'s salary figures come principally from the AAUP.

Regional and local data on faculty compensation are frequently available from state higher education–related boards and regional compacts. Such organizations as the Southern Regional Education Board and the New England Board of Higher Education can provide comparative statistics on professors' income. State agencies, such as the Illinois Board of Higher Education, also provide information that can put individual or average faculty salaries into perspective.

Finally, comparable institutions, such as members of the Great Lakes Colleges Association or department chairs in research universities that compete for the same rather small pool of talent, sometimes share salary data. Of course, it does not require a formal organizational arrangement for a group of colleges to agree to share this kind of financial information.

Data on Professional Variables. Many of the variables needed to evaluate the condition of the professoriate are not as easy to quantify or collect as economic data are. Fortunately, however, information on several other dimensions of professors' work lives is readily available.

Work Load and Faculty Productivity. Many studies have examined the issues of faculty work load and productivity from a variety of perspectives (Fulton and Trow, 1974; Ladd and Lipset, 1975, 1977; Ladd, 1979). The efforts of many institutions to establish equivalencies of work effort across diverse roles have been a failure. To try to develop a formula that will equate a three-hour lecture course with the directing of a play or the supervision of nurses in clinical training is all but impossible. One almost always has to fall back on total time spent in an activity and then make decisions regarding the priority of that activity to the goals of the college.

The *Condition of Education* and the *Digest of Education Statistics* report annually on the numbers of faculty employed full-time and part-time. Numerous studies assessing the average number of hours worked per week are in the literature. Yuker (1974) summarizes these studies. The way in which faculty members divide their time among the classroom, individual student conferences and administrative tasks, research, and professional activities has also been studied extensively (Dunham and others, 1966). Data on the average number of published works (Andersen, 1977) are a common though incomplete measure of faculty productivity. Existing studies show considerable variation in the work distribution and productivity of professors at different career stages and in different fields and different types of higher education institution. Perhaps because of the difficulty of defining and assessing professors' achievements, no national data on professors' productivity are reported regularly. However, data on faculty work loads are routinely monitored by state higher education agencies to comply with legislative accountability requirements. When this information is combined with available national data, it can help to identify trends in the work demands of the academic profession.

Another component of the work load issue is the amount of time that professors commit to work outside their full-time position. The *Chronicle of Higher Education* occasionally presents information on the outside income of college professors ("81 Pct. of Professors," 1981; "Faculty Members' Earnings," 1981). Patton (1980) and Patton and Marver (1979) have also examined faculty consulting practices. There are a number of concerns in this arena. One has to do with institutional policy and desires. Faculty can receive mixed messages in this taboo area. For example, they can receive rewards for keeping the institution in the public eye and simultaneously receive criticism (often indirect) for neglecting their responsibilities to the organization. Another issue has ethical dimensions — who owns what, what resources are being used for personal gain, what rights the organization has in a professor's life after 5:00 P.M. and on weekends, and so forth. And, there is the difficult if not impossible task of collecting accurate information on the subject, especially when the college or university is unclear about its own position and irregular in its practice.

Tenure Ratios. During the 1970s, the percentage of faculty with tenure increased dramatically nationwide (Carnegie Council on Policy Studies in Higher Education, 1980). Annual updates in the *Chronicle,* the *Fact Book for Academic Administrators, The Condition of Education,* and AAUP's annual report on the economic status of the profession make it easy to monitor tenure trends for the American professoriate in general. AAUP also reports tenure differences by institutional type and affiliation, by academic rank, and by sex. The *Fact Book for Academic Administrators* provides additional information by breaking tenure data down by geographic region and type of institutional control (private or public). However, none of these annual reports on tenure presents tenure percentages within specific disciplinary fields.

Age and Rank Distributions. Closely related to the growing number of tenured faculty is the increasing average age of the professoriate. This condition is continually reiterated throughout the higher education literature. The Carnegie Council on Policy Studies in Higher Education (1980) predicts that the age of the modal group of tenured professors, which was thirty-six to forty-five in 1980, will rise to fifty-six to sixty-five in 2000. The *Fact Book for Academic Administrators* gives the age distribution of a 1973 national sample of faculty. These data are divided by sex and institutional type. However, the *Fact Book* does not present aging trends for different disciplinary fields.

Understandably, trends in faculty rank closely parallel trends in age. In recent years, the proportion of college teachers in the upper academic ranks has been increasing. Annual reports in the *Digest of*

Education Statistics and AAUP's annual report on the economic status of the profession present relevant data on this variable.

Faculty Strengths and Weaknesses. No national research on professors' strengths and weaknesses is conducted on a regular basis. Hence, we lack an accurate assessment of the adequacy with which individual college and university faculty members are keeping pace with the knowledge explosion and changing technologies in their field. Several large-scale studies of the American professoriate (American Council on Education, 1972; Carnegie Commission on Higher Education, 1969; Carnegie Council on Policy Studies in Higher Education, 1975; Ladd and Lipset, 1975, 1977) have gathered information on professors' preparation and performance in their numerous roles. Although the reports on these research projects are now somewhat dated, they do provide some useful background on the principal talents and development needs of the professoriate.

Faculty Mobility. Data reported by the Carnegie Council on Policy Studies in Higher Education (1980, p. 80) indicate that the labor market for faculty "has virtually collapsed in all but a few still active fields." The Carnegie Council expects virtually no net additions to the overall professoriate for most of the 1980s and 1990s. AAUP data cited in the annual report on the economic status of the profession shows that the limited growth in higher education is reducing professors' career mobility. Compared with data collected ten years earlier, larger percentages of faculty members at all ranks indicate that they had remained at the same institution during the preceding one-year period ("Surprises and Uncertainties," 1982). Older reports of faculty mobility (Brown, 1967; U.S. House of Representatives, 1965) distinguish among the mobility rates of professors in different fields. The AAUP report only examines the mobility of the profession in general.

Academic Working Conditions. In spite of growing concern about out-of-date equipment and antiquated educational facilities, relatively little information is available on the quality of professors' working conditions. No organization routinely inquires about the general academic work environment, such as the adequacy of office and classroom space or of support for faculty development.

Retirement Plans. Other information that needs to be collected from faculty members over age fifty involves their retirement plans. Not everyone in the academic profession is looking forward to retirement at the youngest possible age that permits a secure future. Rather, the profession probably contains a higher percentage of workers who never wish to retire than any other occupational group. As a rough index, one need simply to note the practice of conveying emeritus status and providing office space to retired staff and then to observe the number of faculty who exercise the privilege.

Of course, faculty first need to know why the data are being sought; otherwise, rumors will spread rapidly that the administration is out to get Jones. No doubt, this data collection is best done on a personal basis. But, because there are now so many options for faculty members formally to end their careers, to make projections for staff needs and possible openings by simply assuming that everyone will retire at age sixty-five can result in large errors. Great variation in the retirement practices and policies between colleges and universities produces options ranging from the early fifties to the current federal law of seventy. Furthermore, policies and practices can be expected to change, as can the law.

Of course, what faculty will say about their retirement and what they actually will do will not always be in complete agreement. That is to be expected. Conditions will change, and changes will affect a professor's future plans. If inflation continues or increases, early retirement (taking sixty-five to be normal) becomes less attractive, essentially impossible for many. If resources improve and salaries begin to increase, more may opt for early retirement. Or, if the environment becomes les stressful and work becomes more pleasurable again, some who planned to leave early may stay on.

A large number of scenarios need to be placed before faculty, who must be asked how likely each seems under certain sets of conditions in an unpredictable future. The resulting data will permit more accurate prognostications than those based on the assumption that all will retire at age sixty-five. Individual faculty plans will need to be updated periodically, or some set of procedures will have to be put in place that will create a climate and a practice that will bring faculty into the right office to tell about changes in their presently registered plans.

Some "buy-outs" have taken place. For the most part, they seem to have been carried out to meet a current emergency, not to build a strong future for individuals and for the institution. Building a strong future is what is needed. If a number of matters related to faculty development should be systematized and attended to on a regular basis, then retirement plans are another element that need to be included. That individual plans can change means that planning will have to be an ongoing process, but that is as it should be.

Data on Personal Variables. The status of academic careers is as closely related to personal variables as it is to economic and professional conditions. Hence, in order to determine the state of the professoriate, it is necessary to examine the personal factors that influence faculty careers. Unfortunately, relatively little relevant information is available. The *Chronicle* occasionally reports on faculty concerns and attributes, such as stress (Fields, 1980) and morale (Soth, 1979). The national faculty surveys mentioned earlier (American Council on Education, 1972; Carnegie Commission on Higher Education, 1969; Carnegie Council on Policy Studies in Higher Education, 1975; Ladd and Lipset, 1975, 1977) provide some valuable data on faculty interests (for example, teaching and research orientations), goals, satisfactions, and attitudes toward other aspects of their work. This information can serve as an instructive baseline for examining the personal career circumstances of professors in 1983. However, because the national faculty surveys are several years old, they cannot give an up-to-date assessment of important factors like professors' satisfaction with their current positions or professors' perceptions of opportunities for career advancement. These studies also cannot indicate the amount of stress that faculty are experiencing under the difficult demographic and economic conditions that prevail for higher education today.

It is unfortunate that many personal dimensions of faculty careers (for example, goals, satisfactions, attitudes toward various responsibilities) are frequently overlooked in efforts to understand the condition of the academic profession. These factors can have an important impact on professors' performance as teachers, role models, scholars, and supportive colleagues. For these reasons, they should be studied on a regular basis.

By way of illustration, asking faculty to report on the percentage of time that they give of their major roles — usually teaching, scholarship, and service — the percentage of time that they would like to give to each, and the percentage allocations that they believe the institution wants can provide valuable information that can be used in a number of ways. First, the data quickly give a work load distribution for a unit.

Second, discrepancies between how faculty actually allocate their time and how they would prefer to spend it provide a good measure of the degree of personal role stress that they are experiencing. Similarly, discrepancies between actual time distribution and what faculty members believe that the organization expects is a measure of job-related stress. Both types of stress can be calculated for each role.

Third, sharing such information with staff can help to address a number of individual and organizational problems. For example, if some faculty want to spend more time in one role and less in others, adjustments can be made to the benefit of both parties and at no cost to the organization. If the imbalance tends to favor one side of the discrepancy (for example, most faculty want to spend more time in research than they do now), the unit can address this as a group problem, not just as an individual frustration. In addition, when faculty see that their colleagues suffer from the same role conflict that they are experiencing, their stress is somewhat reduced.

In these other ways, then, regular collection of such data, which takes little more than five minutes of time, can produce information that can be helpful for individual development as well as for organizational planning.

Relating Faculty Data to Campus Conditions

Each college or university must place information on the condition of the professoriate in proper perspective. National and regional data become useful when they are compared with the attributes and experiences of professors on a specific campus or in a particular academic unit. Institutions that are concerned about the well-being of their faculty members must develop procedures to assess changing local conditions as well as relevant national trends.

An effective system for monitoring the status of faculty requires four principal activities. A person or office is needed to coordinate these activities. First, someone should track national and regional faculty trends by regularly reviewing reports on academic salaries, employment conditions, productivity, and other indicators of the health of the professoriate. The institution should make it standard practice to study periodic reports on faculty, such as those which appear in the *Chronicle of Higher Education* and *Academe* and in publications of the National Center for Education Statistics. Other sources of information on faculty, such as foundation annual reports, higher education journals, and publications from university coordinating agencies, also need to be monitored on a regular basis.

Second, literature and research on important faculty issues — such things as early retirement, faculty redirection, and stress — should be collected and analyzed in depth to assess the relevance of such issues to institutional policies and the careers of individual professors. New issues directly affecting faculty members are always arising. Such topics as collective bargaining and faculty development, which were not part of professors' everyday vocabulary a few years ago, now represent vital professional concerns. Because change occurs at a rapid pace, colleges and universities must try to anticipate and prepare for trends that will influence professors' work lives. Good sources of information on developments affecting faculty include the *Journal of Higher Education, Research in Higher Education, Review of Higher Education, Change* magazine, and publications of the American Council on Education and the American Association for Higher Education. Research reports published jointly by the Educational Resources Information Center (ERIC) and the Association for the Study of Higher Education also help to monitor major developments of concern to faculty.

Third, colleges and universities should regularly compile local data on such key indicators of faculty well-being as salary and compensation, age distribution, tenure percentages, productivity indicators, and faculty development activity. If statistics on faculty members are scattered among various offices on campus, as they often are, it can be difficult to get a clear view of professors' overall state of affairs. However, in order to put national and regional faculty data into perspective, it is necessary to centralize comparable local data. Regular assessment of faculty circumstances, activities, and achievements can help a college to identify developing problems and monitor progress toward important faculty goals. Once an annually updated profile of the faculty presenting salary figures, information on work load, aging trends, outside grants, and research and professional development activity, was set up, it could be maintained fairly easily by an academic administrator or an institutional research office. The benefits of such a profile should outweigh its costs.

Fourth, special studies are needed to learn about local faculty concerns and issues not addressed by national higher education research. The data widely available on the condition of the professoriate present an incomplete picture. A responsible dean or college president would not make policy decisions affecting faculty solely on the basis of the research literature. That information must be fine-tuned with data on the attitudes and opinions of professors on campus. Local research is especially needed on the personal career variables (for example, professors' goals, satisfactions, career problems) that are neglected in most national faculty data banks. Colleges and universities should maintain the capacity to survey faculty opinion on important issues and to monitor trends in the ways in which professors view their responsibilities. On-campus surveys, interviews with individual professors, or brown bag discussions about major faculty concerns are examples of tailor-made research procedures that can give meaning to trends identified in the somewhat sterile reports of government agencies or in national publications.

Conclusion

The available evidence makes it clear that college professors nationwide are working under less than ideal circumstances. However, it would be misleading to conclude that the condition of the professoriate is weak, or lethargic, or even demoralized. The academic profession is not a homogeneous group. Professors' well-being differs among disciplinary fields and among types of higher education institutions. At present, for example, faculty in applied fields like engineering or computer science can choose from many attractive career opportunities. However, professors in the humanities have very limited career options.

To achieve a meaningful assessment of the circumstances and needs of its faculty members, a college or university must keep track of the factors that affect their professional performance. The research on faculty that a liberal arts college conducts will differ in important ways from the studies that a community college or research university will need to carry out. Essentially, higher education institutions must gather the types of information that will help them to maintain an enthusiastic and productive academic work force.

Colleges and universities can profit greatly from careful observation of the condition of the professoriate. Information on faculty well-being can indicate the kinds of support that will be most beneficial to professors at specified points in their career. It can help colleges to develop personnel policies that will foster professors' career growth. It can assist institutions to direct limited financial resources to departments and individuals who will derive maximum benefit from them. Thus, a modest investment of staff time and energy to monitor professors' attributes and needs should pay generous dividends in the form of enhanced faculty morale, growth, and productivity. Close attention to the condition of the professoriate will help higher education institutions to maintain educational vitality by employing their human resources effectively.

References

American Council on Education. *1972 Faculty Study*. Washington, D.C.: American Council on Education, 1972.

Andersen, C. (Ed.). *A Fact Book on Higher Education*. Washington, D.C.: American Council on Education, 1977.

Andersen, C. (Ed.). *1981 Fact Book for Academic Administrators*. Washington, D.C.: American Council on Education, 1981.

Brown, D. G. *The Mobile Professors*. Washington, D.C.: American Council on Education, 1967.

Carnegie Commission on Higher Education. *1969 National Surveys of Higher Education: Faculty*. Berkeley: Survey Research Center, University of California, 1969.

Carnegie Council on Policy Studies in Higher Education. *1975 National Surveys of Higher Education: Faculty*. Berkeley: Survey Research Center, University of California, 1975.

Carnegie Council on Policy in Higher Education. *Three Thousand Futures: The Next Twenty Years for Higher Education*. San Francisco: Jossey-Bass, 1980.

Dunham, R. E., Wright, P. S., and Chandler, M. D. *Teaching Faculty in Universities and Four-Year Colleges, Spring 1963.* Washington, D.C.: U.S. Office of Education, 1966.

"81 Pct. of Professors in Survey Report Outside Earnings Averaging $5,756." *Chronicle of Higher Education,* December 9, 1981, p. 15.

"Faculty Members' Earnings, by Discipline, Beyond Their Basic Salaries in 1980-81." *Chronicle of Higher Education,* December 16, 1981, pp. 6-7.

Fields, C. M. "Faculty Stress Is Found to Be Highest Among Married Women, Single Men." *Chronicle of Higher Education,* September 8, 1980, pp. 1, 6.

Fulton, O., and Trow, M. "Research Activity in American Higher Education." *Sociology of Education,* 1974, *47* (1), 29-73.

Ladd, E. C. "The Work Experience of American College Professors: Some Data and an Argument." In *Current Issues in Higher Education.* Washington, D.C.: American Association for Higher Education, 1979.

Ladd, E. C., and Lipset, S. M. *Ladd-Lipset 1975 Survey of the American Professoriate.* Storrs: Social Science Data Center, University of Connecticut, 1975.

Ladd, E. C., and Lipset, S. M. *Ladd-Lipset 1977 Survey of the American Professoriate.* Storrs: Social Science Data Center, University of Connecticut, 1977.

National Center for Education Statistics. *The Condition of Education.* Washington, D.C.: U.S. Government Printing Office, 1982a.

National Center for Education Statistics. *Digest of Education Statistics 1982.* Washington, D.C.: U.S. Government Printing Office, 1982b.

Patton, C. V. "Consulting by Faculty Members." *Academe,* 1980, *66* (4), 181-185.

Patton, C. V., and Marver, J. D. "Paid Consulting by American Academics." *Educational Record,* 1979, *60* (2), 175-184.

Smith, D. D. "Faculty Vitality and the Management of University Personnel Policies." In W. R. Kirschling (Ed.), *Evaluating Faculty Performance and Vitality.* New Directions for Institutional Research, no. 5. San Francisco: Jossey-Bass, 1978.

Soth, L. "Demoralization of Senior Faculty Members." *Chronicle of Higher Education,* September 24, 1979, p. 21.

"Surprises and Uncertainties: The Annual Report on the Economic Status of the Profession, 1981-82." *Academe,* 1982, *68* (4), 3-11.

U.S. House of Representatives, Committee on Science and Astronautics. *Higher Education in the Sciences in the United States.* Report of the Subcommittee on Science, Research and Development, prepared by the National Science Foundation, 1965.

Yuker, H. E. *Faculty Work Load: Facts, Myths, and Commentary.* Research Report No. 6. Washington, D.C.: ERIC Clearinghouse for Higher Education, 1974.

Roger G. Baldwin is assistant to the provost at Wittenberg University.

Robert T. Blackburn is professor of higher education at the Center for the Study of Higher Education at the University of Michigan.

*Matching faculty with projected staffing needs requires creating
a broad-based inventory of faculty talents and interests.*

Faculty Trends
and Projected Needs

Barbara A. Lee

In order to understand better the extent of the human resources represented by college faculty, it would be useful to construct a profile of
employment trends over the last few decades and to project manpower
needs for faculty over the next few decades. Such a profile would permit planners to analyze the number of faculty in each academic specialization and their current age and employment status. It would also
measure the production of new doctorates each year and would relate
the supply of new doctorates to demand for new faculty. The resulting
profile would be immensely useful for policy makers at the institutional, state, and national level.

However, employment of faculty cannot be analyzed in such a
rational manner because of the free market system that operates in the
United States. That is, we depend on the market's demand for certain
skills or expertise to control the number of individuals who choose to
acquire such training. No government policy regulates how many individuals receive training in a given discipline, although a few federal
programs have attempted to influence individuals to enter a particular
discipline. Although the number of individuals who enroll for specialized graduate training in some areas far exceeds the number of avail-

R. G. Baldwin and R. T. Blackburn (Eds.). *College Faculty: Versatile Human Resources in a Period of Constraint.*
New Directions for Institutional Research, no. 40. San Francisco: Jossey-Bass, December 1983.

able positions, recent graduate enrollment figures in the humanities, social sciences, and law suggest that the free market system does not always operate well for higher education. In addition, changes in enrollment patterns, in terms of the number of students and of the majors that they select, make it difficult for colleges to make long-term projections of staffing needs.

Frequent shifts in federal policy concerning graduate training also complicate efforts to analyze supply and demand for college faculty. In the 1960s, the National Defense Student Loan program created by Title IV of the Higher Education Act of 1965 underwrote graduate training in a wide array of disciplines and provided economic incentives for individuals who entered college teaching. In the 1970s, a number of small federal programs encouraged graduate study in specific areas, such as public service, mining, international studies, and medicine. Later in that decade, federal fellowship programs created by Title IX of the Higher Education Act of 1965 as amended in 1972 provided funds to enable members of minority groups to pursue graduate study in a wide range of disciplines. Funding for most of these federal programs was eliminated in the early 1980s, while the availability of other forms of federal assistance for graduate study, such as federally insured student loans, declined considerably. Thus, shifting federal support for graduate study makes it difficult to predict future supplies of potential faculty.

A third stumbling block in any effort to create an accurate national profile of college faculty is the paucity of data. National-level comprehensive data collection efforts have focused solely on faculty salaries, tenure status, rank, and gender. We have no nationwide data on the age structure of college faculty, the number employed in each discipline, or the productivity of faculty. It is impossible to predict with specificity the retirement patterns of faculty over the next two decades, the number of positions that will be available for new faculty, or the disciplines that, on a national basis, offer the most favorable prospects for new faculty openings.

The National Profile

Despite the shortcomings just outlined, however, it is possible to construct a limited national profile of college faculty. The available data show that the number of faculty has increased steadily over the last decade, that tenure rates are considerably higher, and that the proportion of college faculty who are women or members of minority groups has somewhat increased. The only national-level survey of a census type on college faculty characteristics is conducted by the National Center for Education Statistics (NCES). The most recent data appear in *Faculty Salaries, Tenure, and Benefits, 1980–81* (NCES, 1981).

Number of Faculty. In academic year 1980–81, there were nearly 400,000 full-time faculty in the United States (NCES, 1981). Of that number, about 288,000 (73 percent) were employed at public colleges and universities, while 108,000 (27 percent) taught at private colleges and universities. In 1980, about 124,000 (31 percent) of all faculty taught at universities, 182,000 (46 percent) taught at other four-year colleges, and 90,000 (23 percent) taught at two-year colleges (NCES, 1981).

Overall, in 1980–81, about 105,000 (26 percent) of the full-time faculty were female, an increase from 19 percent in 1970. However, women faculty were not evenly distributed among the several types of institution. Nineteen percent of all full-time faculty at public and private universities were female, while 27 percent of the full-time faculty at other four-year colleges were female. Women were somewhat better represented among community college faculty, where 36 percent were female in 1980–81 (NCES, 1981).

In 1980–81, faculty were fairly evenly divided by rank at the national level. Overall, about 26 percent of all full-time faculty were full professors, 25 percent were associate professors, and 25 percent were assistant professors, while 15 percent of all faculty were employed at institutions that had no academic ranks, primarily community colleges. In fact, slightly more than half of all full-time community college faculty in 1980–81 had no acadmic rank (NCES, 1981).

However, differences among faculty ranks by gender are striking. Overall, only 10 percent of all full professors were women, and only 20 percent of all associate professors were female in 1980–81. In contrast, nearly 35 percent of all assistant professors and 52 percent of all instructors were female. This clustering of women in the lower ranks appears to be a result of recent affirmative action efforts to hire larger proportions of women. This suggests that the cohort of women faculty may suffer a sizable decline if the number of junior faculty required at a number of colleges and universities is reduced.

While data describing full-time faculty are limited, data related to part-time faculty are virtually nonexistent. It has been estimated that 32 percent of all faculty teaching in colleges and universities in 1980 were employed on a part-time basis. Between 1972 and 1977, the number of part-time faculty increased by 50 percent, while the number of full-time faculty increased by only 9 percent ("The Status of Part-Time Faculty," 1981). Community colleges rely most heavily on part-time faculty; in community colleges, more than half of all faculty are employed on a part-time basis ("The Status of Part-Time Faculty," 1981). Use of part-time faculty affords administrators flexibility in meeting staffing needs without committing the institution to a long-term investment in an individual faculty member. Part-time faculty members are also less costly to hire, for they usually are paid on an hourly basis or at a per-course rate, which is often far below the per-course equivalent salary of full-time faculty, and their fringe benefits are limited or nonexistent. However, from the perspective of full-time faculty members, the use of part-time faculty creates numerous problems. Part-time faculty often do not participate in institutional governance, curriculum development, or student counseling. They are often excluded from the bargaining unit of full-time faculty at unionized colleges, because their employee interests are different from those of full-time faculty. Heavy use of part-time faculty blurs the employment picture for college faculty overall, it denies usually well-qualified part-time faculty the opportunity to be full participants in the academic community, and it increases the governance and counseling responsibilities of full-time faculty.

Tenure Status. The numbers and proportions of tenured faculty are of particular significance in a time of fiscal stress for colleges and universities, such as the present. Program change or initiation is extremely difficult at a college with a high proportion of tenured faculty, for an institution must declare a state of financial exigency before it can legally lay off tenured faculty ("The Dismissal of Tenured Faculty," 1976). Similarly, a high proportion of faculty with tenure often means that turnover within a college's faculty will be minimal and that there will be few opportunities for new blood to mix with the static faculty membership.

On the national level and across institutional types, the proportion of tenured faculty is not yet alarmingly high. In 1980–81, 65 percent of all full-time faculty were tenured. At public institutions, 68 percent of all faculty were tenured, while at private institutions, 56 percent of all faculty were tenured (NCES, 1981).

However, tenure rates show some differences by type of institution. On the national level, 66 percent of all full-time faculty at public universities were tenured in 1980–81, while 60 percent of full-time faculty at private universities were tenured in that academic year. Sixty-five percent of all faculty at public four-year colleges and 65 percent of the faculty at private four-year colleges were tenured that year. Tenure rates were highest at public two-year colleges (75 percent) and lowest at private two-year colleges (just under 50 percent) (NCES, 1981).

The tenure status of college faculty varies substantially by gender. In 1980–81, on the national level, 70 percent of the male faculty and just under 50 percent of the female faculty were tenured. At private universities, 37 percent of the women faculty and 66 percent of the men faculty were tenured; at public universities, the proportions were 43 percent and 71 percent respectively. Similar disparities are evident at four-year colleges: In 1980–81, 37 percent of the female faculty and 60 percent of the male faculty at private colleges were tenured, while respective proportions were 50 percent and 71 percent at public colleges. Tenure rates were closer at two-year colleges: In 1980–81, 68 percent of the female faculty and 79 percent of the male faculty at public two-year colleges were tenured, while 40 percent of the female faculty and 57 percent of the male faculty at private two-year colleges were tenured (NCES, 1981).

Few surveys have been conducted to determine the tenure rates of minority faculty. However, data collected by the Equal Employment Opportunity Commission (EEOC) in 1977 showed sizable disparities between the tenure ratios of white and minority faculty: While 68 percent of the white faculty were tenured overall in 1977, only 51 percent of the black faculty members, 58 percent of the Hispanic faculty, and 60 percent of the Asian faculty were tenured in that year (EEOC, 1980).

Tenure rates by rank vary primarily at the assistant professor level and below. At universities, 15 percent of all assistant professors and about 5 percent of all lecturers and instructors were tenured in 1980–81. At other four-year colleges, 30 percent of all assistant professors, 7 percent of all instructors, and 18 percent of all lecturers were tenured. (These proportions reflect primarily figures for public colleges; tenure rates for junior faculty at private four-year colleges were similar to those for universities). However, at two-year colleges, 60 percent of all assistant professors, 22 percent of all instructors, and 36 percent of all lecturers were tenured in 1980–81 (NCES, 1981).

While the overall tenure rate for faculty at all senior institutions (universities and four-year colleges combined) in 1980 was 65 percent (NCES, 1981), the proportion of tenured faculty at senior institutions was only 50 percent in 1970 (Carnegie Council on Policy Studies in Higher Education, 1980). Two-year colleges were not included in those estimates. The Carnegie Council has projected that tenure rates at the senior institutions will peak at 77 percent 1986 and then decline through retirements and resignations to 67 percent by the year 2000 (Carnegie Council, 1980). These projections imply that the number of new faculty positions will become increasingly limited over the next two decades. They also imply limited mobility for senior tenured faculty.

Age Structure of Faculty. To date, no publicly available nation-wide survey has been conducted to determine the age structure of college faculty. Such data would be immensely useful to policy makers and planners at the state and national levels as a partial indicator of the longevity of the faculty glut in some disciplines, and they would aid in predicting the health of the faculty job market over the next two or more decades.

Two national surveys of a stratefied sample of faculty conducted nearly ten years apart show that the average age of college faculty has increased. In 1969, Bayer (1970) found that approximately one half of the faculty in his sample were under age forty. In 1978, a survey by the Carnegie Council on Policy Studies in Higher Education of a similar sample of faculty found that just over one third of all faculty were under-age forty (Carnegie Council, 1978). The Carnegie Council (1980) estimated that the modal age of tenured faculty in four-year colleges and universities would be between thirty-six and forty-five in 1980, between forty-six and fifty-five in 1990, and between fifty-six and sixty-five in the year 2000. If the federal law forbidding mandatory retirement before age seventy continues to be applied to colleges and universities, the steadily rising tenure rates mean that opportunities for young professionals to join college and university faculties will be severely curtailed.

Production of Potential Faculty. An analysis of the production of doctorates provides only a rough measure of the number of potential faculty members, since many individuals who receive doctorates take jobs in business, industry, or government and do not wish to hold a faculty position. Others pursue the degree because it is required for the practice of their profession. Nonetheless, it is fair to state that a sizable proportion of individuals who earn the doctorate probably would like to enter college teaching at some point in their careers.

The relationship between production of doctorates and the health of the faculty job market is evident when one examines trends over the last two decades. In 1960, about 9,700 individuals received degrees. By 1967, that number had more than doubled (to 20,400), and in 1970 about 29,500 doctorates were awarded. The number of doctorates awarded annually peaked in 1973 at 33,756 and then declined over the second half of the 1970s; it stood at 31,319 in 1981 (National Research Council, 1982).

While the overall production of doctorates has decreased since 1973, the number of doctorates awarded in certain fields has declined very little, and it has even begun to rise again. In life sciences, engineering, and physical sciences, doctoral production has increased slightly over the last few years. However, in the social sciences, humanities, and education, overall declines have been substantial (National Research Council, 1982).

Trends in the production of doctoral degrees have differed sharply by gender over the last decade. While the total number of doctoral degrees has declined nearly every year since 1973, the number of such degrees awarded to women has increased every year, from 4,596 in 1971 to 9,862 in 1981 — an increase of 115 percent. The largest numerical increase was in the field of education, where the number of women receiving doctorates annually is already reaching — and may soon surpass — the number of men. The number of women receiving doctorates in the physical sciences increased by 47 percent between 1971 and 1981, in engineering by 560 percent, in the life sciences by 102 percent, and in professional fields (including business administration) by 140 percent (National Research Council, 1982). The number of women receiving doctorates in the humanities declined between 1977 and 1981, but the 1981 figure still represents an increase of 31 percent over the level in 1971 (National Research Council, 1982).

Comparable data are not available for the production of doctorates by ethnic group. However, figures for 1981 show that the proportion of doctorates earned by all nonmajority ethnic groups (with the exception of Asians) is extremely low. For example, with the exception of the field of education, where blacks received 9 percent of the doctorates in 1981, blacks received between 1 and 5 percent of the doctorates awarded in every field. For Hispanics, the percentages ranged from 1 to 3. (The high of 3 percent was in the humanities.) For Native Americans, the percentages were less than 1 percent (National Research Council, 1982). Clearly, members of most ethnic minority groups are still severely underrepresented among holders of doctoral degrees.

However, the progress of women and ethnic minorities in obtaining doctoral degrees may appear less laudatory when we consider the ability of those who wish to gain employment in academe to do so. Nearly half (44 percent) of all persons who received doctorates in 1981 planned to be employed in academe, and 18 percent planned postdoctoral study, which suggests an orientation toward research and scholarship. Yet, 20 percent of all recipients of the doctoral degree in 1981 were still seeking employment at the time when they completed their degree. In disciplines where women and minorities tend to earn a higher proportion of doctoral degrees — social sciences, the humanities, and education — the proportions of new doctoral recipients still seeking employment were well above the average of 20 percent (National Research Council, 1982).

Implications of the Faculty Profile. While the national picture of

America's college faculty is blurred in some respects and incomplete in others, it is clearly a mixed one. New scholars are still being trained, although in smaller numbers than they were a decade ago, and more than half either wish to be employed in academe or are honing their research or professional skills for future academic employment. Thus, while the new generation of scholars may have diminished as a result of the weak job market for college faculty, it has not been destroyed.

However, one might well question whether optimism is justified for much longer. Tenure rates at four-year colleges and universities are projected to increase to near saturation levels within a very few years. The average age of faculty will be around fifty before 1990. Most colleges have yet to feel the full impact of enrollment declines, which demographers expect to have their greatest impact in the early 1990s (Carnegie Council, 1980). The small and recent gains in the proportions of women and minority faculty achieved during the late 1970s may be reversed if junior faculty are laid off in response to fiscal pressures and student enrollment shifts into newly popular disciplines.

However, the national picture is both too broad and too blurred to be useful to faculty and administrators in planning for the future of a particular institution. The picture at an individual institution may be quite different, and solutions must be based on the problems that characterize the particular college. Therefore, it is more useful for planners to collect and analyze data that will describe trends and product projections for a specific institution in a particular locale.

The Institutional Profile

What kind of information does a college have about its faculty? More important, what kind of information does a college need to have about its faculty? Are institutions using information that they already possess to assist them in planning? How can they collect useful information about their faculty?

Many institutions began to address these issues years ago and now possess sophisticated reporting systems and data banks that provide a profile of faculty characteristics. Employment records can supply basic personal data. They are also a source of information on additional areas of faculty expertise, such as prior training or job experience in a different field. Some institutions require productivity reports, both as a monitoring device for accountability pruposes and as an incentive to greater productivity. However, much more information would be useful to institutional researchers and others involved in the planning process.

There is little doubt in the minds of most planners that colleges will need to tap their faculty for an ever wider range of skills and talents over the next two decades. As faculty grow older and more highly tenured, a college may need to ask faculty to do more than simply to teach four or five courses a year in their disciplinary speciality. At some colleges, curricular change and innovation may depend on the ability of faculty to perform other tasks, to teach in areas outside their narrow focus, or to work with groups beyond the campus. These colleges will not be able to use their faculty more creatively unless they have information about where and how each faculty member can contribute.

Colleges interested in creative uses of faculty should build an information bank that includes data on areas of faculty expertise beyond the field in which the terminal degree was earned. Faculty may hold the master's degree in fields other than their doctoral specialization. Furthermore, some may have taken the trouble to remain reasonably current in their master's degree discipline. Other faculty may have work experience in areas that would equip them to teach in a discipline other than that of their terminal degree. A simple questionnaire and brief interviews would enable planners to collect such information on the hidden resources of college faculty.

Other data would also be useful. Would the faculty member be willing to retrain or to take refresher courses in another discipline, either at his or her own expense or at the college's expense? Would the faculty member be willing to accept part-time administrative duties? If so, in what areas of administration? Is the faculty member able and willing to develop cooperative programs or partnerships with outside agencies, both public and private? Could the faculty member initiate, organize, and supervise a joint industry-college training or research project? Would the faculty member be willing to act part-time as a student recruiter? These questions only begin to suggest the kinds of information that planners could use to help shape the future direction of their college.

Information on the talents and skills of individual faculty could be integrated into overall institutional planning. Student enrollment trends and shifts in enrollment patterns by discipline or major would ordinarily raise the threat of staff reductions in departments in which enrollment declines substantially. While such reductions may ultimately be necessary, combining projections of enrollment shifts with information from the enriched data bank on college faculty could suggest alternative solutions that would not otherwise have emerged. The proportion of full- and part-time students and projections for future enrollment patterns by part-time status could also be analyzed in light of the enriched data base. Students' postgraduate plans (employment versus graduate training) could influence the staffing of certain courses and modify the curriculum as well.

One limitation on a college's flexibility in using faculty in new and different roles is imposed by a collective bargaining agreement between faculty and administration. This contract may limit the number of courses that a faculty member may teach, or it may guarantee a certain course load. The contract may forbid or discourage faculty from assuming administrative responsibilities. If the contract stipulates that seniority is the only consideration in decisions about termination of faculty, administrators may not be able to use faculty in new roles. Indeed, such a stipulation might actually force more layoffs than a more flexible contract would have required. Understandably, faculty members desire job protection and fair treatment, especially when staff reductions are threatened. There may not be sufficient trust on campus to permit administrators and faculty to work together to use as many faculty as possible in ways that will benefit the college, the faculty, and the students. However, the hard times predicted for higher education in general, which a number of institutions are already experiencing, suggest that cooperation and flexibility, rather than rigid bilateral agreements, will best serve the employment interests of faculty.

One area of obvious interest to institutional planners is retirement trends among the college faculty. What are the present trends? How will they be affected by college efforts to comply with the Age Discrimination in Employment Act that permits faculty to teach until age seventy? What is the age structure of the present faculty, and how will it affect future retirement trends? If the college wishes to do so, how can its current institutional policy be modified to encourage early retirements without committing an excessive amount of the college's resources?

Data collection on all these issues could result in several benefits. Besides developing a more comprehensive portrait of the richness of the college's faculty resources, the resulting information would suggest areas of faculty development for some individuals and new responsibilities for others. The mere collection of such information might serve as an incentive for some faculty to engage in new activities or to update their skills in areas of former interest. Of course, not all faculty would wish to participate in activities beyond their own research and teaching, and others might lack the breadth of skills or interests that would permit them to assume other duties or accept new fields of teaching. These limitations argue all the more forcefully for the importance of a complete and broadly based data bank on college faculty so that multitalented individuals and those willing to accept new challenges can be identified, their abilities can be capitalized on, and their cooperation can be rewarded.

Planning for Future Needs

It hardly bears repeating that careful long-range planning is essential to an institution's health and in some cases to its survival. Projections of student enrollment over the next five or ten years are often the most significant and sometimes the only data used in long-range planning. The enriched faculty data base described in this chapter would enhance planning and permit planners to integrate the talents of faculty already employed to help shape the college's future.

Planners will try to determine what the college will look like in five, ten, or twenty years if no interventions are made. They may also try to describe what the college community would like the college to look like ten or twenty years into the future. After developing these scenarios, planners could then estimate their impact on present faculty. How many will still be employed at the college in ten years? In what disciplines will faculty supply exceed student demand? How many new faculty will be required and in which areas? What state-level regulations or practices, such as program review or program evaluation, might affect college programs? It is often at this point that the planning and projecting halts, and steps are sometimes taken to reduce or eliminate programs or shift curricular emphases.

Layoffs of faculty may be necessary no matter how creative an institution is in its planning. However, the enriched data base may permit the college to identify and use the talents and interests of faculty who might otherwise lose their jobs. The data base may also help to identify faculty members whose skills would be valuable in the planning process itself, as well as those who should be included in the college governance process. In short, integrating the faculty data base into the long-range planning process can only enhance both the process and the outcome for faculty and college alike.

Colleges can use the enriched data base to help them to utilize faculty more productively or to cope with necessary program reductions in ways that will not result in faculty unemployment. A recent program at New York University sponsored by the Ford Foundation prepared individuals with doctorates in the humanities to assume positions as business executives. Other institutions could inaugurate similar programs, beginning with their own faculty, who could then, as adjunct instructors employed by business in executive or managerial positions, train other faculty. Thus, the college could reduce its faculty, train them for alternate employment, and then use them to institute a new training program that could train faculty from other colleges for non-academic careers.

Another alternative that the enriched data base suggests involves developing arrangements that allow faculty in low-demand disciplines to combine academic with nonacademic employment. The result would not be simply two part-time jobs for a faculty member. He or she could remain a full-time college employee at his or her regular salary, or a bonus could be paid, and the college could enter into a long-term contractual agreement with a private business or public agency for the faculty member's services. Such a venture would permit the college to make staff reductions and benefit from the resulting cost savings without laying off faculty. A similar plan might combine teaching and administrative duties for certain faculty members who might otherwise be laid off.

Some planners believe — not unwisely — that faculty productivity must be increased to meet the increasingly tight financial circumstances that more and more colleges face. Merely increasing faculty course loads or requiring faculty to perform more research will not address the complex problems created by declining and shifting enrollments and by changing employment patterns for college graduates. Creative solutions are needed, including the modification of reward systems to encourage faculty to be flexible and to seek out new skill areas and new responsibilities. Such activities as extrainstitutional projects, industry-university cooperation, and retraining can be rewarded with financial incentives, enhanced job protection, or added prestige.

Individuals who have completed graduate training and who have chosen the academic route are talented, energetic, intelligent people. There are many ways in which colleges can respond to fiscal pressures and make necessary organizational changes without terminating faculty. Between the extremes of shaping the faculty to fit the college and shaping the college to fit the faculty lies the opportunity to shape both the college and its faculty by recognizing the wider talents and interests of faculty, the broader potential of the college, and the way in which both can be integrated.

References

Bayer, A. "College and University Faculty: A Statistical Description." *ACE Research Reports,* 1970, *5* (5).

Carnegie Council on Policy Studies in Higher Education. *Three Thousand Futures: The Next Twenty Years for Higher Education.* San Francisco: Jossey-Bass, 1980.

Equal Employment Opportunity Commission. Unpublished data, 1980.

Higher Education Act of 1965, Public Law 89-329.

National Center for Education Statistics. *Faculty Salaries, Tenure, and Benefits, 1980 – 81.* Washington, D.C.: U.S. Department of Education, 1981.

National Research Council. *Summary Report 1981: Doctorate Recipients from United States Universities.* Washington, D.C.: National Academy Press, 1982.

"The Dismissal of Tenured Faculty for Reasons of Financial Exigency." *Indiana Law Journal,* 1976, *51,* 417–432.

"The Status of Part-Time Faculty." *Academe,* 1981, *67* (1), 29–39.

Barbara Lee is assistant professor in the Graduate School of Education at Rutgers University, where she teaches higher education, law, and administration courses. Formerly, she conducted research on college faculty for the U.S. Department of Education and the Carnegie Foundation for the Advancement of Teaching.

Colleges and universities faced with budgetary problems or personnel supluses may be able to use career change or early retirement incentives to encourage faculty members to leave the institution.

Institutional Practices and Faculty Who Leave

Carl V. Patton

The problems that academe faces today are many and varied. They have been documented by numerous authors, and they are being experienced firsthand in one form or another by faculty members of virtually every college and university in America. As a consequence, it is not necessary to repeat the litany of problems here except to note that increasing numbers of academics and would-be academics no longer see a career in academe as the route to success and happiness (Gottschalk, 1982; Lovett, 1980; Solmon and others, 1981). A substantial minority of today's middle-aged academics are both interested in leaving academe and believe that they would be as happy or more happy with a career outside academe (Palmer and Patton, 1981). At the same time, early retirement remains attractive to older faculty members who, for a variety of reasons, would rather not continue in academe (Palmer and Patton, 1981; Patton, 1979; Toevs and Hanhardt, 1982). Furthermore, many colleges and universities are finding that they cannot afford to pay their faculty because of declining enrollment and reduced funding levels, not to mention the problems created by an imbalance between student demand and faculty staffing. These problems have encouraged colleges and universities to devise ways of assist-

R. G. Baldwin and R. T. Blackburn (Eds.). *College Faculty: Versatile Human Resources in a Period of Constraint.*
New Directions for Institutional Research, no. 40. San Francisco: Jossey-Bass, December 1983.

ing faculty members who want to leave academe and of encouraging others to leave so that more drastic measures, such as involuntary termination, pay cuts, and furloughs, can be avoided.

Practices focusing on leavers can be helpful to the instutition. If these practices are properly designed and thoughtfully administered, they may help the institution to save funds, they may allow disaffected personnel to leave gracefully, and they may permit resources to be shifted to areas of new demand. These practices may even improve the quality of teaching, research, and service if wise hiring decisions are made and if needs and trends can be anticipated. Moreover, career change options and early retirement programs are attractive to faculty members who wish to follow other career paths but who need support and encouragement to make a move that both flies in the face of many years of education and training and that conflicts with the beliefs held by colleagues and friends.

More than 200 colleges and universities have some form of early retirement or career change program ("Labor Letter," 1981), although many include only minor inducements and are not very well developed. Nonetheless, career change options and early retirement incentives are becoming increasingly popular. Some observers believe that they will become more widespread in academe now that age seventy has become the mandatory retirement age. If mandatory retirement is abolished entirely, such incentives may become even more attractive as ways to induce turnover that can open up space and funds for faculty members with needed skills and attributes. This chapter gives an overview of career change options and early retirement incentives and alerts the reader to policy implications and implementation issues, options, and incentives.

Most retirement plans permit faculty members to retire early if they are willing to take a reduced annuity. Since some faculty members interested in early retirement cannot afford to take a reduced annuity, a number of institutions have found ways of increasing the annuities of persons who wish to retire early. Supplemental annuities, one-time severance payments and part-time postretirement employment have been used to supplement the early retirement pension. The cost of the incentive can be recovered by not filling the vacated position, by delaying the refilling, or by hiring a less expensive replacement.

While such schemes can work for faculty who are nearing retirement age, they are too expensive or they provide too small an incentive for persons at midcareer. Thus, the incentive concept has been modified to appeal to the needs of faculty at midcareer. The career change incentive most central to the concerns of this chapter is that intended not to enable faculty members to assume new assignments in the same institution but to prepare faculty members for a position outside the institution. The cost of the career change option is justified in the same way as the early retirement incentive. The funds are recovered by not replacing the faculty member, by delaying the replacement, or by hiring a less expensive person.

A variety of early retirement incentives and career change options have been established in American colleges and universities. I have categorized these schemes in earlier work, most recently in *Academe* (Patton, in press), and I will summarize those options in this chapter. The type of scheme best suited to the particular institution will depend on several factors, including whether the institution has a defined benefit or defined contribution retirement plan, whether the institution has an above-average or below-average percentage of faculty members at midcareer or nearing retirement, and whether the institution has the ability to model faculty turnover and to calculate the direct and indirect costs of various options. These differences notwithstanding, the description of early retirement and career change incentives that follows should enable an institution to begin to evaluate the various options.

Early Retirement Incentives

Five types of early retirement schemes have been used in business, industry, and academe (Jenny, 1974; Patton, 1979). They can be used individually or in combination, and they can be modified to respond to institutional idiosyncracies. The five basic incentives are: early retirement benefit payments larger than actuarial tables would justify, lump-sum severance payments, annuity enhancements, phased retirement or reduced employment, and continuation of perquisites.

Liberalizing the Actuarial Reduction. Not fully reducing the early retiree's pension to compensate for the lesser amount paid in and the longer period during which benefits will be received is a common incentive. This option typically involves an across-the-board increase in all early benefits. However, the increase is modest, and it is usually not enough to encourage many people to retire early.

Lump-Sum Severance Payments. The lump-sum severance payment option involves a direct cash payment to an employee who elects to leave before the normal retirement date. The incentive, typically equal to one or two years' salary, can be paid in a lump sum or spread out over one or two years. The early retiree also receives an early retirement pension if he or she is eligible for one under the basic retirement program.

Annuity Enhancements. Early retirement income can be increased to the amount that the faculty member would have received if he or she had waited until the normal or retirement plan target age to retire. This increase can be accomplished either by providing an annuity that supplements the early retirement annuity or by providing an interim payment that permits a delay in the date when the faculty member begins to collect on his or her regular retirement annuity, thus increasing eventual monthly payout.

In the first instance, the faculty member retires early and begins to draw an early retirement pension. During the period between early retirement and the normal retirement age, the institution supplements the early retiree's pension with cash payments from his or her old salary line while at the same time purchasing with funds from the same source a supplemental annuity to go into effect at the normal retirement age (Patton, 1979). When the supplemental annuity goes into effect, the direct cash payments cease.

In the second case, the annuity is enhanced by postponing the date when it is taken, thereby producing a larger annuity (White, 1981). At institutions with a defined contribution pension plan, such as TIAA–CREF, where benefit levels are determined by accumulations in individual accounts, the faculty member can retire early and begin receiving social security income but delay taking the pension until he or she reaches normal retirement age. During the period between early retirement and the normal retirement age, the institution pays the early retiree the difference between the social security benefit and an income objective. The interim cash payment can be financed out of the early retiree's old salary line. This second technique works only where the early retiree will receive social security income or income from a pension in addition to the income from the college or university and for defined contribution plans. Colleges and universities that do not participate in social security and that have defined benefit plans where benefit levels are not determined by accumulations in individual accounts should explore the annuity supplement arrangement.

The financial objective of these options can be set in a number of ways. The total annual retirement benefit (early annuity plus supplement or social security benefit plus interim payment) can be set to equal the expected annual benefit at normal retirement, a percentage of this amount, a percentage of preretirement salary, and so forth. Alternatively, the pension supplement can be set as a function of the median preretirement salary or the median expected annuity for the early retiree's age-service cohort (Hopkins, 1972). This provides a greater financial incentive to retire for persons receiving below-average compensation. The argument is that persons paid salaries that are lower than average are less valued in relation to peers and hence more suitable candidates for early retirement.

Phased Retirement. The phased retirement option may become more popular as early retirees seek ways to hedge against inflation and ease into retirement. Like the supplemental pension option, this arrangement is intended to assure a retirement income approximately equal to what the retiree would have received if he or she had not retired early. The phased retirement option can take the form of a reduced workload and a corresponding reduction in pay (Furniss, 1981), or the option can combine a supplemental annuity and reduced or part-time employment (Patton, 1979). In either case, the percentage of employment can be reduced by a fixed amount at the outset, or it can be reduced gradually over several years.

Under the supplemental annuity and part-time employment arrangement, the faculty member retires, begins to draw the early retirement annuity, and then is rehired on a part-time basis for one or more years. Income from the part-time employment supplements the early retirement benefits. In addition, the college or university purchases a supplemental annuity that will take effect at the normal retirement age, so the early retiree's total pension will not be reduced by the early retirement. Both the part-time position and the supplemental pension can be financed from the faculty member's existing budget line.

Perquisites. Benefits and privileges have been provided by colleges and universities to ease the transition to retirement. Early retirees have been provided special memberships in the faculty club, reduced ticket prices to campus events, campus parking privileges, library privileges, computer access, and in some cases laboratory, studio, or office space and secretarial assistance.

Career Change Options

Although early retirement incentives can take many forms, some institutions or fields may find that early retirement will not serve their needs. The effectiveness of the option varies among colleges and universities, depending on the salaries and work histories of candidates, the configuration of the basic and supplemental pension schemes, the discount rate used to calculate the present value of benefits, changes in life-table values, and so forth.

Programs have been devised to encourage younger people to leave academe, thus freeing funds or opening positions for faculty members with needed skills. Formal career change options in academe include those intended to enhance performance in a current role or a closely related new role and those intended to lead to a position outside academe. Some schemes address both objectives. Several colleges and universities have launched career assistance efforts. Typical programs are aimed at encouraging faculty members to develop career plans (Baldwin and others, 1981; Barry and Naftzger, no date; "Ca•reer Re•new•al," 1980). In addition to sessions on goal setting, growth plans, and financial planning, some programs include workshops for people who want to prepare for a shift to employment outside academe. Another approach permits faculty members to undertake as much as one year of study in a related discipline, with the intent that the new knowledge will be incorporated into the faculty member's teaching and research (Broudy, 1978).

These career assistance efforts address an important need in academe, and, with help, some faculty members can shift to another position within their current institution. However, there is also a need to shift faculty members to jobs outside academe: It is likely that fewer faculty positions will be available in the future, some academics may not be good candidates for internal shifting, and recipient departments may resist the crossover. Several approaches have been used to encourage career shifting.

Retraining for Outplacement. Programs have been devised to assist faculty members in departments with declining enrollments to develop new skills. Faculty members who enter these programs receive their regular salary plus a grant to finance graduate study. The programs have varied, but they generally cover tuition costs, relocation costs, and other associated expenses. Retrainees undertake programs lasting from one semester to one year. They have studied in entirely new disciplines as well as in allied specialties within their existing disciplines. A few have earned advanced degrees. Although these programs have benefited individual faculty members and helped existing talent to be better used, they have encouraged only a few career shifts.

A more recent and apparently a more successful outplacement effort is part of a comprehensive career development program. The program includes career assessment and skills development workshops and an option that permits faculty members to experiment with alternative employment. During participation in the career development program, faculty members may decide to attempt a temporary outplacement in business, government, or a nonprofit setting. At the end of one year, the participant decides whether he or she wishes to return to the university (Barry and Naftzger, no date). Approximately half of the individuals placed have chosen to leave the university permanently.

Emerging mid-career outplacement options include variations of the retraining schemes just described plus the severance payment concept (Palmer and Patton, 1981). Faculty members who elect to terminate at mid-career can be provided with a paid leave plus retraining costs, or faculty members who take a position elsewhere can be provided for a limited period with a payment that equals the difference if any between the old and the new salary.

Paid Retraining. A professor too young to consider early retirement can be paid to undertake retraining for a position outside academe. The faculty member agrees to terminate after retraining. Consider the following example: An associate professor who earns $30,000 a year accepts a package that includes full pay for one year ($30,000), tuition and fees ($6,000), travel and relocation expenses ($4,000), and a severance payment ($10,000) in exchange for termination at the end of the following academic year. If the changer is not replaced, the $50,000 can be recovered through the unfilled salary line in less than two years. If the changer is replaced immediately by a lower-salaried person, the cost takes longer to recover — six years in the case of replacement at approximately three fourths of the changer's salary. This simple calculation ignores the fringe benefits that may be continued during the retraining, since these costs vary greatly among institutions. Furthermore, the individual institution may wish to set the inducement higher or lower, and the length of the retraining period can also vary.

Earnings Supplement. This mid-career severance arrangement involves an agreement between a college or university and a career changer to pay the difference, up to a fixed proportion, between his or her present faculty salary and the salary of the new position. The differential payment is limited to a given period; perhaps three years, and it can be reduced each year. For example, the university or college could guarantee up to 100 percent of the career changer's salary for the first year, up to 75 percent for the second year, up to 50 percent for the third year. In the case where a $30,000-per-year associate professor takes a $20,000-per-year position and a 100 percent differential is guaranteed for three years, the subsidy can be recovered in one year if the changer is not replaced. If the changer is replaced immediately with a person at three fourths of the former salary, the supplement can be recovered in four years. This computation excludes fringe benefits, since they will be provided by the new employer.

Policy Issues

Before adopting early retirement or career change incentives, colleges and universities must consider a number of policy issues.

Among these issues is whether the incentives will appeal to the better teachers and researchers. Some evidence suggests that the options appeal to persons who are already interested in leaving academe and to faculty members who rate themselves as less successful than colleagues (Palmer and Patton, 1981) as well as to those who are less active in funded research and publication (Palmer, 1979). These findings are derived from national data collected before the recent increase in the mandatory retirement age and before the dramatic increase in the inflation rate in the late 1970s. However, more recent studies are obtaining similar results. Early retirement incentives appeal to the disaffected, and they do not appeal disproportionately to faculty members who consider themselves to be the better teachers (Toevs and Hanhardt, 1982). Informal reports from colleges and universities now implementing early retirement or career change options suggest that the general thrust of these findings still applies. However, individual institutions must use the national data and the findings from other institutions with caution. For example, when the national data are examined by field or otherwise disaggregated, the relationships tend to weaken. Furthermore, the national data do not permit analysis of faculty beliefs by individual institution. Institutions that devise policies regarding potential leavers should certainly be guided by national data, but they would be wise to collect data about their own institution.

Institution-specific data are important for addressing another question: Will early retirement incentives or career change options be effective? That is, are there potential candidates for these options at the given institution? National data show faculty members distributed by age in a pyramid-like form; the bulk of faculty members are found in the younger age categories, with decreasing numbers in each older age category (Patton, 1979). At some institutions and in some fields, a bulge may be found at the older ages. Such bulge may suggest that there are enough faculty mmbers in preretirement cohorts to make the development of early retirement incentives worthwhile. For institutions with few persons in these categories, early retirement incentives make little sense. The same dilemma may exist for mid-career change incentives, but most institutions have the bulk of their faculty members in the middle age cohorts. Nonetheless, if individual institutions are to approach the development of incentives for leavers intelligently, they must examine their age profiles and estimate how the age distribution by field will change in the future. If institutions find that they have few near-retirement faculty members, an early retirement incentive scheme would have little impact, and it would not be worth the implementation cost. Or, they may find that the prevailing retirement and termination rates indicate that modifications in staff structure will correct current, temporary maldistributions.

Institutions must also be aware that incentive schemes have essentially a one-time impact; that is, they accelerate the prevailing termination or retirement rates by encouraging people who would leave in coming years to leave slightly earlier. This means that colleges and universities that implement career change or early retirement incentives must be willing to trade an increase in the near-term resignation or retirement rate for a decrease in that rate in the future. To put it another way, if faculty members are induced to leave earlier than normal, they will not be present to affect the retirement or resignation rate in the year when they would have retired or resigned.

Costs must also be weighed in developing policies for potential leavers. The options incur both direct and indirect costs. Direct costs include the cost of the supplemental annuity, the severance or retraining payment, and the benefits or perquisites that may be continued for the employee who leaves. Indirect costs include not only personnel costs involved in designing and implementing the options but also intangible costs, such as the effort involved in negotiating policy changes, the persistence it takes to get faculty and administrators to tackle the problem, and the effort required to overcome institutional inertia. These problems should not be blown out of proportion; many colleges and universities have dealt with them successfully. However, the issues should be faced early, and the institution must be convinced that the results are worth the effort and that the staffing changes brought about by these incentives will not create problems in the future.

Implementation Considerations

Some faculty members are definitely interested in career change or early retirement incentives. If an institution wishes to capitalize on that interest, the administration must design and implement the scheme with a number of considerations in mind. For example, faculty members now changing careers are finding jobs outside academe (Feinberg, 1982; Gottschalk, 1982; Lovett, 1980; Solmon and others, 1981), but an increase in career changers may reduce job availability. An institution may therefore have to provide job counseling and job search assistance. Potential early retirees may also be reluctant to retire because they perceive the need for laboratory or studio space. Others may simply need or want a university or college mailing address and a minimal continuing relationship with the institution. The key ingredients to successful career change or early retirement incentives will vary by institution, and institutions that are serious must gauge faculty interests and requirements. This suggests that some type of consultation with faculty is needed during design and implementation, either through a survey of attitudes or through input from a representative committee. At the same time, the institution must develop a capacity for coping with the change introduced by these schemes. A faculty flow model can be of great assistance here. At least a basic model should be developed, one that incorporates historical data on retirement and outmigration rates and policy data about tenure-granting practices, hiring priorities, and career change and early retirement incentives. A more sophisticated model would include a cost component to estimate the fiscal impact of each option. At a minimum, the institution should project future states under a continuation of past trends and estimate minimum and maximum changes that could be expected under the options being considered. Examples of options and assistance are available in a number of publications (Bleau, 1981, 1982; Grey, 1980; Hopkins and Massey, 1981; Jenny, 1974; Jenny and others, 1979; Patton, 1979; White, 1981) and from annuity carriers. Institutional counsel will also have to be consulted during the design and implementation phases, as these incentives may encounter tax regulations and age discrimination laws.

Most incentive schemes involve the continuation of some faculty benefits. While benefits and perquisites alone will not induce academics to leave, they are essential ingredients of an incentive package. Colleges that provide tuition remission may decide to continue the benefit for family members of career changers who are already attending the institution. The tuition remission can be continued until the faculty member completes the career change or until the dependent completes the course of study, whichever occurs first.

Health and disability coverage are important concerns for career changers. Thus, the institution may choose to continue coverage of these benefits during the career transition period and permit the leaver to purchase coverage until it becomes available from his or her new employer. Institutionally provided life insurance can also be provided through the transition phase, with the career changer being permitted to continue the coverage at his or her own expense.

In some institutions, departmental or division resistance will have to be overcome. Although implementation procedures vary among institutions, departments or program chairs often are centrally involved in arranging early retirements or career shifts. If departments find that vacated positions are being recovered by the central administration, chairs may be reluctant to expend the effort to negotiate a career shift or an early retirement. However, department chairs may realize that they will have to return a position in the long run, and thus they may elect to obtain it in this way. Alternatively, they may desire to postpone the event as long as possible. In order to overcome such resistance, some institutions have decided to return part of the vacated position to the generating unit in the form of a part-time position, teaching assistance support, or operating expenses. Of course, high-demand areas may be permitted to refill the position, although perhaps at a lower and less expensive rank.

Career change incentives appear to be most helpful to a college or university if they can be targeted at areas most hard hit by enrollment decline. However, targeting incentives may run afoul of age discrimination laws and raise questions about coercion on the part of the institution. Instead of such targeting, colleges and universities are making these options available to all employees with the expectation that faculty members in declining fields will be those most likely to respond. If acceptance rates prove to be similar among high- and low-demand fields, the college or university can reallocate the vacated positions to respond to institutional needs and policy. This approach would reduce the possibility of charges that the college or university was interfering with the rights of employees.

When devising incentives, an institution needs to clarify the focus or purpose of such programs. Are they to encourage retirements or terminations? Are they intended to improve the skills of currently employed faculty members? Are they to help cut expenses? Are they intended to respond to shifting student demand? Institutions would do well to avoid the temptation to say yes to all four questions. Rather, the central purpose of the incentives should be decided, and well-conceived options should be implemented. Faculty support for such options must be engendered, and perhaps the best way to do this is to have the faculty senate or another representative body centrally involved from the outset in the design and development of the incentives.

The career change and early retirement incentives outlined here may be more attractive and easier to implement for some institutions than they are for others. Large institutions may find that these options are relatively easy to implement, because their large faculty body means that terminations will average out among programs and departments. Small colleges may find that the induced terminations cluster in several small units where immediate departures could be disruptive. However, the small colleges may also find that career change programs are relatively easy to establish because consensus is relatively easy to achieve. Private colleges may also find implementation less difficult, because they are not faced with the question of using public funds to pay people to terminate. All these problems can be resolved, however. Timing and phasing of retirements and terminations and the use of visiting faculty members can ease the transition problem in small colleges. Severance payments have been offered at public institutions under the rationale that they save funds in the long run and that the faculty members who take them are exchanging future economic return from continued employment for current income.

Sufficient information is now available that colleges and universities can develop career change options and early retirement incentives. However, such efforts can be relatively meaningless if they are developed in isolation from a larger plan for institutional vitality. The design of such options should be hand in hand with a reassessment of other personnel practices. For example, information about the basic retirement program and faculty benefits can be made more available and perhaps more understandable. These efforts can also lead to faculty review and evaluation mechanisms, improved career and retirement counseling, enhanced treatment of emeriti, and improved understanding of institutional dynamics—knowledge that is becoming increasingly important as colleges and universities cope with today's financial constraints, declining enrollments, and shifting student demand. The development of effective career change options demands attention and effort from campus leaders and administrators. Whether they can find the time and energy for this activity while trying both to recruit students and to keep the budgetary wolf from the door remains to be seen.

References

Baldwin, R., and others. *Expanding Faculty Options: Career Development Projects at Colleges and Universities.* Washington, D.C.: American Association for Higher Education, 1981.

Barry, R. M., and Naftzger, B. *Career Development Program.* Chicago: Loyola University, no date.

Bleau, B. L. "The Academic Flow Model: A Markov-Chain Model for Faculty Planning." *Decision Sciences,* 1981, *12,* 294–309.

Bleau, B. L. "Faculty Planning Models: A Review of the Literature." *Journal of Higher Education,* 1982, *53,* 195–206.

Broudy, H. S. *Faculty Study in a Second Discipline,* unpublished report, Advisory Committee on Interdisciplinary Programs, University of Illinois, Urbana, 1978.

"Ca·reer Re·new·al." In *PROD,* newsletter of the Pennsylvania State College, Educational Services Trust Fund, Winter 1980.

Feinberg, L. "The Retrofitting of the Ph.D." *Washington Post,* July 19, 1982, pp. 1, 5.

Furniss, W. T. *Reshaping Faculty Careers.* Washington, D.C.: American Council on Education, 1981.

Gottschalk, E. C. "Some Frustrated Humanities Ph.D.'s Find Success After Being Retrained for Business." *Wall Street Journal,* December 16, 1982, p. 27.

Grey, P. "A Faculty Model for Policy Planning." *Interfaces,* 1980, *10,* 91–103.

Hopkins, D. S. P. *An Early Retirement Program for the Stanford Faculty: Report and Recommendations.* Stanford, Calif.: Academic Planning Office, Stanford University, 1972.

Hopkins, D. S. P., and Massey, W. F. *Planning Models for Colleges and Universities.* Palo Alto, Calif.: Stanford University Press, 1981.

Jenny, H. H., Heim, P., and Hughes, G. C. *Another Challenge: Age Seventy Retirement in Higher Education.* New York: Teachers Insurance and Annuity Association, 1979.

Jenny, J. R. *Early Retirement, a New Issue in Higher Education: The Financial Consequences of Early Retirement.* New York: Teachers Insurance and Annuity Association, 1974.

"Labor Letter." *Wall Street Journal,* June 9, 1981, p. 1.

Lovett, C. M. *Difficult Journey: Senior Academics and Career Change.* New York: Baruch College and Graduate School, City University of New York, 1980.

Palmer, D. D. "Faculty Responses to the Higher Mandatory Retirement Age: Which Faculty Members Will Stay?" Paper presented at the Midwest Economics Association Meeting, Chicago, April 6, 1979.

Palmer, D. D., and Patton, C. V. "Mid Career Change Options in Academe: Experience and Possibilities." *Journal of Higher Education,* 1981, *52,* 378-398.

Patton, C. V. *Academia in Transition: Mid Career Change or Early Retirement.* Cambridge, Mass.: Abt Books, 1979.

Patton, C. V. "Voluntary Alternatives to Forced Termination." *Academe,* in press.

Solmon, L. C., and others. *Underemployed Ph.D.'s.* Lexington, Mass.: Lexington Books, 1981.

Toevs, A. L., and Hanhardt, A. M., Jr. "The Effect of Early Retirement Incentives on Faculty Quality." *Collegiate Forum,* 1982, *?,* ??-??.

White, G. W. "Bridge over Troubled Waters: An Approach to Early Retirement." *Journal of the College and University Personnel Association,* 1981, *32* (2), 8-12.

Carl V. Patton is dean of the School of Architecture and Urban Planning, University of Wisconsin–Milwaukee. His recent research in higher education includes early retirement and career change incentives, consulting practices of academics, and faculty involvement in extended education.

Faculty members have the capacities for work and change that can contribute to maintaining institutional quality despite budget cuts. Together, faculty members and administrators can create environments that release energy.

Faculty as a Renewable Resource

Wilbert J. McKeachie

The resources of colleges and universities are limited. In most institutions, these resources have been declining. In some institutions, budgets have shrunk; in most institutions, budgets have not kept pace with inflation. Nevertheless, despite the budget cuts, the reductions in capital expenditures, and the contraction in numbers of faculty, one major institutional resource still has elasticity—faculty time and energy. Although in discussion with already overworked colleagues there will be cries of protest if one says that faculty work load is expandable, one can stand by that claim.

Time is not unlimited, but it makes a substantial difference whether faculty members spend thirty-five hours or seventy hours a week on university work—and thirty-five to seventy hours does not even represent the full range of current faculty effort. Some faculty members seem to work fewer than thirty-five hours a week. Many work more than seventy—not as a result of some outside pressure but because they enjoy their work.

Not only do faculty represent a resource with some elasticity, they are also a resource that is renewable. We hear a great deal these days about mid-life crises, academic menopause, the crisis of the aging faculty, the harmful consequences of the tenure system, and the need to get rid of dead wood. All these catchwords represent stereotypic

R. G. Baldwin and R. T. Blackburn (Eds.). *College Faculty: Versatile Human Resources in a Period of Constraint.*
New Directions for Institutional Research, no. 40. San Francisco: Jossey-Bass, December 1983.

beliefs about the downward course of vitality and productivity among mature faculty. Of course, the facts themselves are not nearly as frightening.

Aging

What do we know about aging? What happens biologically, psychologically, sociologically — and most important, what happens to performance? Those who teach about aging are sometimes prone to an overly optimistic view of the joys of old age. An optimistic view is merited, but we cannot deny that there are real declines in certain functions. Vision, hearing, reaction time, and sensorimotor functions generally decline in later life. Fortunately, people can compensate for losses in some of these functions, and most of these losses have little impact on academic performance.

There are also hormonal changes with age. For men, adrenalin and noradrenalin decline after about age fifty, and there are changes in the testosterone and estrogen balance for both men and women. Again, these changes interact with environmental changes in ways that make it difficult to link them directly with changes in performance. There are great individual differences, and the hormonal changes associated with aging seem to be strongly affected by psychological and social influences.

What about psychological changes? Probably the area of most concern to academicians is that of intelligence. Here, the news is generally good. Not too long ago, it was believed that one hit one's intellectual peak in the late teens or early twenties and that everything went downhill from there. This generalization was based on cross sectional studies that assessed the intelligence of people of different ages without taking sufficient account of the fact that education varied across the generations. When individuals who had first been tested in the years after World War I were tested thirty years later, the findings were quite different. The scores increased with age. In the last ten or twenty years, many studies of intellectual changes with age have been conducted, and it appears that verbal intelligence — the abilities involving vocabulary and information — tend to increase to quite an old age. A professor will probably score higher at age eighty than he or she did at age twenty. Intellectual abilities involving novel materials — such things as reorganization of figures or shapes — probably begin to drop off in the fifties. One of the factors at work in the apparent decrease in this kind of ability is probably practice. Abilities that we use and practice seem to be maintained rather well; abilities that are not practiced tend to drop off. Thus, individuals who are skilled in a particular area, such as a scholarly discipline, and who have continued to work in that discipline, continue to improve or at least to maintain a high level of ability. We tend not to practice abilities that are not well developed; thus, they are likely to decline. Rubinstein, Picasso, Casals, and others had remarkable ability at an advanced age. Studies of chess masters point to an important generalization. High levels of performance in older people do not necessarily mean that their abilities have simply increased or stayed level. Frequently, these people have adopted new strategies that make less demand on declining abilities, and they make effective use of the abilities that are maintained.

Another area related to aging is attitude toward time. For a good part of our lives, we think of time in terms of age since birth. Children will volunteer: "I'm three going on four." In the academic world, we frequently think of time in terms of the years since we earned our Ph.D.: "He got his Ph.D. ten years ago, but he seems a little slow in getting out his publications." At some point in our life, we change from counting the years since birth or since the Ph.D. to counting the years left. Whereas the academic career seems to stretch without limits in one's younger days, hitting age sixty can have a psychological impact that leads one to think about how many years are left. Obviously, such a change has important consequences for one's attitude and motives.

Sociological changes are also important as we think about aging faculty and faculty renewal. Older persons and younger persons are expected to play different roles. A young person's comments can be excused as those of one who is bright and bumptious but who lacks experience. The older person is expected to be the voice of experience, displaying wisdom and judgment; silly comments from an older person are likely to be interpreted as signs of impending senility. Older faculty members are more likely to be asked to take on administrative work, to serve on committees, to act as mentors, and to assume other roles that tap their experience and presumed wisdom. These are not unproductive activities. Effective use of human resources implies drawing on faculty strengths, and assignment to mentorships or important committees can be a very useful way of challenging an individual to develop new interests and new enthusiasms. But, the roles that we expect older people to play have some negative aspects as well. Young chairpersons are often unwilling to challenge the right of older faculty members to continue teaching "their" course although the course may no longer be needed or need to be rejuvenated. Often, a chairperson is unwilling to ask older faculty members to take on tasks that they performed in the past but that are seen as beneath the dignity of older persons. Thus, an individual who was once a successful teacher at the undergraduate level may be restricted to graduate-level teaching because the introductory courses are typically taught by graduate students and assistant professors. The result is likely to be that the older person gets in a rut that provides little stimulation and few challenges.

My review of biological, psychological, and sociological changes with age has already dealt with some aspects of faculty performance. What is the evidence of the relationship between age and faculty performance in teaching and research? With respect to teaching, the major source of evidence are studies of student ratings of older and younger faculty. There are relatively few data following individual professors over their career. As a result, most of the data are derived from cross sectional studies that compare younger and older faculty members. The general finding is that student ratings are lower for teachers in their first year or two of teaching but relatively unrelated to age after that. Contrary to the common belief that faculty members stop trying once they have achieved tenure, teaching effectiveness seems to be maintained. The perception that there are large numbers of faculty members who are completely ineffective is contradicted by such data as those from University of Michigan studies which show that 90 percent of faculty are rated as excellent teachers by the majority of their students. There is no evidence that large numbers of faculty members are perceived by their students as dead wood.

Similarly, with respect to research productivity, Pelz and Andrews (1976) found that productivity does not drop off after tenure is attained. In their studies of research productivity, both in academic settings and in large research organization, Pelz and Andrews found two peaks, one in the late thirties and early forties and one in the late fifties. In a recent national study, Astin (1983) found that the youngest and the oldest faculty members were the most productive. Once again, we find no evidence of major losses of effectiveness with age.

This review of the evidence on aging leads to two major conclusions. First, individuals differ greatly, and these differences are likely to increase with age, so that generalizations about older faculty are generally not applicable to all individuals. Thus, in looking at faculty as a resource we should look at individual cases, not at age groups. Second, individuals have the ability to change at all ages. At one time, it was common to hear that personality, intelligence, and other basic individual characteristics were fixed by age five and that human development was characterized by continuity and stability. Today, life span development research has shown that there is much less continuity in the lives of individuals than we once believed. Where continuity and stability are found, they are often the results of a relatively constant environment, not of inherent rigidity. Individuals retain a remarkable capacity for change all through their life.

Continuity and stability among older people may often result from acceptance of stereotypes about age by older persons themselves. How many times have we heard an older person say, "I'm too old to change now" or "It's too late to start something new now"?

Challenging the stereotypes does not imply that we should close our eyes to real problems. Individual faculty members differ in their productivity. They differ from one another, and they differ from time to time. Sometimes, faculty members joyfully work seventy to eighty hours a week. Other times, they grudgingly do little more than meet their classes. Sometimes, they are thinking of new and better ways of teaching, are creative in their research, and are helpful in solving the university's problems. At other times, they teach the conventional material, depend on their students to do their research, and doze through committee meetings. What are the conditions that make the difference? First, let us look at some of the negative factors, then at some positive things that contribute to productivity — things that administrators might consider if they wish to enhance faculty productivity or to renew faculty resources.

Dead Wood

As already indicated, dead wood is both rare and real. Probably everyone knows one or two faculty members who have somehow failed to achieve the promise that they seemed to hold when they were promoted to tenure and who seem to have given up trying to achieve normal academic goals. To deal with this problem, we need to think about why people become dead wood. Nobody intends to become dead wood, and nobody enjoys being perceived as dead wood.

We can gain some understanding of the problem if we look at some factors that influence careers. Ochberg (1983) studied men in the middle years of life in relationship to their career. Ochberg sees the career as a resolution of basic personality needs, some of which go back to problems arising in early childhood. A career represents choices that enable the individual to cope with conflict, but the resolution can become shaky if it fails to satisfy all the needs in conflict. Ochberg uses the concept of career trajectory. In our culture, advancement in a career is important, and public signs of advancement are markers by which we judge our progress. We build up a sense of momentum that carries us forward from one marker to another. For assistant professors, a major goal is achieving tenure. As a consequence, the current heavy emphasis on high research productivity and concern about competition with one's peers can diminish research productivity in the long run and take much of the fun out of a long-term academic career (McKeachie, 1982).

However, even those who achieve tenure do not always sustain their momentum. According to Braskamp and others (1982), most faculty members, after achieving tenure, seek a balance between professional and personal goals. They become able to work toward more distant goals. But, the slope of advancement can be too steep for some. Accidents occur. Ten percent of adults have a major illness or injury that makes it hard for them to work. Interpersonal events intervene. Braskamp and others (1982) found that family and personal relationships are very important to faculty members. One factor that diminishes stress among academics, according to French and others (1982), is that professors feel that their family and friends value their work. Thus, when marital conflict, divorce, family illness, or death of a spouse intervenes, energy is sapped, and the whole career trajectory can slope downward. Problems with children, children's health, children's school problems, or behavioral problems can also absorb energy. One wonders whether Levinson's (1978) forty-year-olds experiencing mid-life crisis had teenage children with special problems. Sometimes, one problem leads to another; instead of a temporary plateau or drop in one's productivity, things go from bad to worse. Obviously, events at home interact with events on the job. Good family relationships can facilitate the release of energy on the job, just as a person happy in work can be a happier and more effective family member.

Moreover, stress on the job can decrease productivity. Department chairs or administrators who are critical and unappreciative of good work, incompatible colleagues, a sense of not being respected or appreciated for what one is doing — all these can lower the faculty member's involvement in work. While the transition from associate professor to full professor is not usually viewed as being as critical as the transition from assistant professor to associate professor, individuals whose promotion is delayed or who do not make full professor are likely to lose their enthusiasm for their job and to displace their energy onto other activities. In some cases, such hobbies as golf, tennis, or card playing absorb the faculty member's time. In other cases, energy is used more constructively in positions of community service. In still other cases, individuals devote themselves to outside consulting or moneymaking activities or even to committee work within the university. Such displacement activities are not unique to academia. Heckhausen (1980) studied German business executives and found a similar phenomenon among many executives who reached the end of their advancement before achieving the presidency.

The discouragement and sense of lack of worth of those who are stopped short of the full professorship suggest that productivity could be improved if everyone were promoted to full professor after a reasonable period of time. In many ways, the dead wood phenomenon can be explained by Seligman's (1975) theory of learned helplessness. Originally, the learned helplessness phenomenon was observed in dogs who, after experiencing a series of uncontrollable shocks, were no longer able to learn to avoid shock as normal dogs did. Even in situations that required only minimal movement, such as walking from one part of the cage to another, the dogs simply cowered and prepared to receive the shock; they did not attempt to escape from it. Seligman (1975) suggested that individuals who experience a number of failures are likely to develop a tendency to give up and feel depressed. As further research tested this theory with human beings, it became apparent that it is not so much the experience of unhappy events but the effect of events on our expectations for the future that is crucial. That is, if we perceive that a particular failure experience indicates a decline in our abilities or a change in the situation that points to an undesirable future, it is likely that we will become depressed and give up.

Failure experiences are not uncommon these days. Today's faculty members, who were recruited in the 1950s and 1960s during the period of expansion, were promoted to full professor at a time when there were many graduate students and when teaching loads were relatively light and involved largely graduate teaching. The drop in graduate admissions, the need for undergraduate teaching—which previously was seen as unworthy of mature scholars—and the cutbacks in research grants, together with the bleak national economy and predictions about dark days ahead for higher education, can all create an expectation that the future is not going to be as bright as many dreamed in their early days as academicians. It takes only a couple of grant proposal rejections to lead one to wonder whether one is still competent. Poor student ratings for a few classes can lead one to question one's ability to maintain rapport and to understand and work effectively with students. It may not take very many such events to produce the loss of energy that is symptomatic of the dead wood phenomenon.

Renewing Faculty Energy

How can faculty energy and creativity be maintained and renewed? Most studies report that older faculty are more diverse than young faculty. As already indicated, individuals tend to become increasingly different because we tend to practice and enjoy the things that we do well and not to practice the things in which we experience relatively less success; as a result, our ability in these areas declines. Older faculty members are likely to vary greatly not only in productivity but also in interests, abilities, roles, and career patterns. Thus, any general prescriptions should be taken not as recipes to be administered uniformly. Instead, they should be used as guidelines for individual prescriptions. The research studies of Pelz and Andrews (1976), Clark and Corcoran (1983), and Blackburn (1982) provide some useful clues about the kinds of conditions that can release faculty energy.

Freedom. Almost every study of faculty motivation indicates that individuals who go into academic life choose it because of strong needs for autonomy. Studies of university faculty in various stages of their career report that faculty members value autonomy and stress their freedom and sense of personal control of their life as an important element of their satisfaction. This does not mean that administrators should adopt a laissez-faire philosophy. The optimal freedom is freedom within an organization that has goals of its own and coordinates faculty goals in ways that help to accomplish institutional goals.

Diversity. Pelz and Andrews (1976) indicate that faculty do well when they have opportunities to do more than one thing. A full-time researcher is not likely to be more productive than the faculty member who combines research with administration or teaching. Thus, while one wants to use the special competencies of faculty in order to maximize individual ability, one does not want to take away other demands and opportunities.

One is reluctant to say a good thing about budget cuts, but it may well be that current fiscal constraints will force colleges and universities to make new demands on older faculty. At the same time, these new demands may actually help to revitalize those who have grown stale doing the same thing year after year. Faculty members need opportunities for growth. Team teaching assignments, working with other faculty members to develop new courses, encouragement to develop new skills — these can all increase satisfaction and productivity. Senior faculty members recognize and appreciate opportunities for learning.

Risk Taking. Productivity in the later years of academic life is most likely to be maintained if faculty members are encouraged to take on new projects, to take risks rather than settling into comfortable patterns. One problem posed by the older faculty member is that both the faculty member and administrators are likely to feel that it is not worthwhile to ask the older person to prepare a new course or to conduct research requiring the development of new skills since there are only a few years left to retirement. Perhaps the potential end of mandatory retirement will reduce these conservative pressures.

Complexity. Faculty members report that they would like to see more emphasis on teaching and that they would like to have more time to spend on teaching. One reason for these reports can be that the teaching situation offers new challenges and a complexity that is continually stimulating. Faculty members are stimulated by seeing differences that they had not observed among students and among teaching approaches that work with different kinds of students. As they observe their teaching and their students more closely, new complexities and new questions emerge that help to maintain stimulation and challenge. In the national surveys of occupations by French and others (1982), faculty members scored high in their desire for complexity and reported that academic life provides very nearly the optimal amount of complexity.

Time Pressure. One common complaint of younger faculty members is the excessive time pressure that they feel. Administrators should be aware of these problems and be sensitive to the need to help younger faculty members control the demands on their time or at least to develop time management strategies.

In contrast, administrators are sometimes reluctant to apply time pressures to senior faculty. Many department chairs are reluctant to ask senior professors to take on more work or to assume roles that are different from those that the professor has filled in the past. As I argued earlier in this chapter, it is not healthy for older faculty members to hold tightly to "their" courses. Some rotation of courses is probably good both for faculty members and for their students.

Conclusion

What can we conclude from this summary of conditions leading to loss of energy and of conditions conducive to increased investment of energy? There is always hope. Moreover, administrators can manipulate the environment in ways that enable individuals to find hope in the situation. Like other human beings, faculty members can do a great deal to construct their own environment. They are curious, they like to feel competent, and they work hard when they feel that they are making a worthwhile contribution. A sense that they are appreciated for their contributions, a feeling that the future has bright spots, a sense that they are valued by their colleagues and by administrators—these are

66

things that will improve the effectiveness of faculty members. Faculty members need to have a sense of the high expectations and confidence that we place in them. Usually, our younger people have a sense that we expect much of them, but older faculty may well feel that, while we appreciate their past contributions, our expectations for their future contributions have diminished. Both younger and older people need to sense that they are being encouraged to do well, to work hard and effectively. A faculty career can still be fun, just as it has been fun in the past.

References

Astin, H. "Faculty Incentives and the Underprepared Student." Paper presented at the annual meeting of the American Association for Higher Education, Washington, D.C., March 1983.

Blackburn, R. T. "Career Phases and Their Effect on Faculty Motivation." In J. L. Bess (Ed.), *Motivating Professors to Teach Effectively.* New Directions for Teaching and Learning, no. 10. San Francisco: Jossey-Bass, 1982.

Braskamp, L. A., Fowler, D. L., and Ory, J. C. "Faculty Development and Achievement: A Faculty's View." Paper presented at the annual meeting of the American Educational Research Association, New York City, April 1982.

Clark, S. M., and Corcoran, M. "Professional Socialization and Faculty Career Vitality." Paper presented at the annual meeting of the American Educational Research Association, Montreal, April 1983.

French, J. R. P., Jr., Caplan, R. D., and Harrison, R. V. *The Mechanism of Job Stress and Strain.* New York: Wiley, 1982.

Heckhausen, H. "Motive-Dependent Crises of Successful Business Executives in Middle Age." Unpublished paper presented at the Social Science Research Council, Committee of Life-Course Perspectives on Middle and Old Age, meeting on "Self and Personal Control of the Life Span," New York, New York, October 6, 1980.

Levinson, D. J. *The Seasons of Man's Life.* New York: Ballantine, 1978.

McKeachie, W. J. "The Rewards of Teaching." In J. L. Bess (Ed.), *Motivating Professors to Teach Effectively.* New Directions for Teaching and Learning, no. 10. San Francisco: Jossey-Bass, 1982.

Ochberg, R. "Middle-Aged Men and the Meaning of Work." Unpublished doctoral dissertation, University of Michigan, 1983.

Pelz, D. C., and Andrews, F. M. *Scientists in Organizations.* (Rev. ed.) New York: Wiley, 1976.

Seligman, M. E. P. *Helplessness.* San Francisco: Freeman, 1975.

Wilbert J. McKeachie is professor of psychology and director of the Center for Research on Learning and Teaching at the University of Michigan. His research and intellectual interests have dealt with college teaching and the psychology of aging.

Even in a period of constraint, retrenchment, and adjustment,
we must not forget the importance of ongoing renewal for our
most important resource, the faculty who stay, most of whom
will be part of the academy for many years to come.

Faculty Who Stay: Renewing Our Most Important Resource

William C. Nelsen

Throughout this volume, faculty are seen as versatile human resources in a period of constraint. The focus of this chapter is on faculty who stay in our higher education institutions, most of them for many years to come. How can we assist these faculty to be versatile human resources in a period of constraint? Three words in that question are essential: *versatile, resources,* and *constraint.*

First, faculty are versatile. Just like students, faculty members differ in their interests and in their needs. Yet, this simple fact is often overlooked by those who design programs for faculty development and renewal. Because faculty are versatile in both talents and attitudes, faculty will not all respond to a single approach to development. Some faculty will respond assertively to opportunities for research grants, other will not. Some faculty will seldom if ever take part in a discussion concerning classroom teaching; others will be excited about and benefit greatly from such discussion. For some faculty, an individual grant for research or field study is an important stimulus for renewal; for others, working with colleagues in an interdisciplinary approach to development is more effective. In order to take advantage of the versatility of faculty members, faculty development programs themselves must be versatile and multifaceted.

R. G. Baldwin and R. T. Blackburn (Eds.). *College Faculty: Versatile Human Resources in a Period of Constraint.*
New Directions for Institutional Research, no. 40. San Francisco: Jossey-Bass, December 1983.

Second, faculty are important resources. As a result of the need for retrenchment that many colleges and universities have faced in recent years, a great deal of attention has been given to the questions of early retirement and of preparing faculty to make transitions to other professions. While there is clearly a need to focus on such matters, we must not forget that faculty who stay will continue to be our most important educational resource. These faculty deserve our attention, and we must make sure that we have effective programs in place to ensure their continuing renewal and development.

Third, we are operating in a period of constraint. Can programs for faculty renewal be maintained or started despite the constraints of the 1980s? Throughout the past decade, a great deal of time, energy, and money was spent to develop programs for faculty renewal. Many programs were initiated with the encouragement and assistance of foundation and federal government grants. Can such programs be maintained without outside resources in difficult economic times? The experimentation of the 1970s teaches that, while some programs were too expensive, a wide variety of faculty development programs could be started and maintained at relatively low cost. Thus, the answer to the question, can we renew versatile human resources in a period of constraint? is a resounding yes. We can, and we must.

Faculty Renewal: More Important Than Ever

Clearly, faculty development has been a major emphasis of colleges and universities throughout the past decade. Concerned about an aging, less mobile faculty and spurred on by financial support from foundations, federal government agencies, and often internal budgets, colleges and universities created a wide variety of new approaches to faculty development. These new approaches were both many and varied. They provided opportunities for summer study and release time, and they created centers for teaching improvement or instructional development, new forms of student and peer evaluation, short-term workshops in institutes on special topics concerning both scholarly content and new approaches to teaching, faculty growth plans, internships for faculty in areas relating to their discipline, faculty exchanges, and mentorships programs for senior and junior faculty. In addition, the more traditional approaches of sabbaticals, special leaves, and travel to professional meetings were adopted on some campuses, and they received increased attention on others. For descriptions of these old and new approaches, see Bergquist and Phillips (1975, 1977, 1981), Centra (1976), Freedman (1973), Gaff (1975, 1978), and Lindquist (1979).

The problems that sparked the concern for faculty development programming have actually become more acute, but in typical American fashion we have become tired of concentrating on this particular subject, and we have turned our attention to others. Yet, recent conversations by this author with a wide variety of people in colleges and universities indicate that most campuses are still struggling with the issue of how to create and maintain effective programs for faculty renewal. While it will be difficult to undertake new programs, especially expensive programs, in the coming years, there is little question that faculty renewal is now more important than ever. Four reasons are especially important.

First, faculty mobility has decreased. Mobility in colleges and universities began to decrease in the 1970s, but some movement was still taking place. Now, however, despite our efforts to devise early retirement options and to promote movement out of the academy to other professions, it is clear that the 1980s will not witness an influx of new faculty into the profession. Many colleges will be facing dificult periods of retrenchment. Faculty development programs for those who remain will be more important than ever.

Second, faculty morale is threatened. During a recent visit to a college campus, this author heard a college president remark: "We must do all that we can to prevent college teaching from becoming the depressed profession during these coming years." During periods of retrenchment, there is great danger that faculty morale will suffer and that retrenchment will turn into entrenchment; that is, that we will turn in on ourselves and fail to adapt to a changing world as we compete for scarce resources. A careful, well-thought-out process of adjustment within our institutions can prevent this reaction from occurring. An ongoing, exciting, enriching faculty development program can be extremely important in keeping our educational programs alive and lively, even during difficult times.

Third, new findings on adult and student development bear attention. Throughout the late 1960s and the 1970s, the body of literature concerning adult development (Levinson, 1978; Sheehy, 1974) and student development (Perry, 1968; Heath, 1968; Chickering, 1969; Astin, 1977; Katz, 1968) was much enriched. Most faculty development programs created during those years either came too early or failed to take many of these important findings into account. New understandings of the changes in various stages of adult life have major implications for efforts to encourage faculty personal and professional renewal. In only scattered instances have faculty development programs drawn on the findings of student development researchers.

Knowing how students grow and change intellectually, socially, and emotionally during the college years can have profound implications for approaches to teaching. Faculty development programs can encourage significant renewal by challenging faculty to reexamine both course content and pedagogical approach in light of these new findings.

Finally, institutional needs, especially the challenges of a period of constraint, are pressing. In the next several years, institutions will be forced to make major adjustments to changing enrollment patterns as well as to new curricular needs. Moreover, colleges and universities by and large will have to call on existing resources, not new ones. This will mean that many faculty will have to take on new assignments in order to fill in the gaps or to meet curricular needs dictated by a changing society. An active faculty development program can help faculty to assume new challenges and help institutions to alter size and program.

Programs in Faculty Renewal: What Is Needed and What Works

Faculty development is not a narrow concept. One of the problems that we face in the academy is that too many persons, especially faculty themselves, have had a very narrow view of the possibilities for renewal. For some, faculty development has mean only teaching improvement. For others, it has meant only the traditional means of renewal, such as sabbatical leaves or funds to attend professional meetings. *Faculty development*, as the term is used here, means all the activities designed to improve faculty performance in all aspects of their professional lives—as teachers, scholars, advisers, academic leaders, and contributors to institutional decisions.

The project on faculty development that the author directed on behalf of the Association of American Colleges (AAC) divided faculty development activities into four categories: professional development—scholarship, improved research skills, broadening of scholarly areas; instructional development—improved teaching skills, new teaching techniques; curricular change—development of new courses, significant changes in current offerings, development of interdisciplinary courses; and organizational development—introduction of new campuswide policies promoting faculty development, focus on campuswide goals, development of new committee systems, reward structures designed to encourage faculty renewal.

Faculty development must be seen not only as broad in approach but also as broad in the variety of lives touched. No one, no matter how good, should be exempt from participation in faculty renewal activities, for the moment one stops growing as a person or a professional, he or she begins to die. Growth ought to be constant for everyone throughout life.

Given this broad understanding of faculty development, we must then ask what is really needed in faculty development programming and what works. These were the questions that the AAC study of faculty development activities in twenty colleges around the country addressed. Nelsen and Siegel (1980) provided examples of effective programs in each of the four categories just mentioned, while Nelsen (1981) presents an extensive, personal analysis of the important issues in creating effective programs of renewal. Seven guidelines for meeting current needs in faculty renewal with programs that work emerge from the AAC research.

First, a multifaceted, flexible approach is best. As this volume stresses, faculty are versatile human resources. Faculty development programs must therefore respond to versatility, not to sameness. Colleges that have instituted only a single form of faculty renewal have ordinarily reached only a small portion of the faculty. Colleges that have tried a more flexible approach seem to have reached more faculty and to have done so to more lasting effect. To the extent possible, faculty development programs must provide a variety of opportunities — for research, teaching improvement, curricular change — and a variety of approaches — individual grants, group study projects, exchange programs, released time, and so forth. Only in this more flexible manner will a significant number of faculty be affected.

Second, individual activity in faculty renewal must be balanced by corporate activity. Because faculty are versatile, it is important to have opportunities on campus for individual responses. This has been the most typical method of developing and renewing people — through sabbaticals, professional travel assistance, released time, and individual grants. Such opportunities can be very effective. Even small, well-administered grants can have a very important effect on an individual faculty member. In the course of an interview, a faculty member who had just received a $300 grant remarked, "This is the first time that I have ever received a grant for anything that I was doing in my teaching." Despite its modesty, this recognition had a very positive effect on the faculty member, as it encouraged him to do some useful research and to try a new approach to teaching.

Nevertheless, individual approaches to faculty development must be balanced by corporate activities that give faculty members an opportunity to work closely with colleagues and take broad institutional and curricular goals into account. The process in which faculty members work for their renewal with other colleagues can be important for a number of reasons. For example, individualized approaches to faculty renewal tend to encourage faculty compartmentalization. That is, if a college puts all its faculty development funds into individualized activities, such as summer study grants, released time, or special travel, it can actually encourage intellectual divisions among faculty. This is particularly counterproductive if the institution is working to create interconnections in the curriculum. In the past several years, a number of colleges (Nelsen and Siegel, 1980; Nelsen, 1981) have emphasized corporate faculty development programming. The result has been an improved intellectual interchange among faculty, a stronger sense of what can be gained from colleagues both within and outside one's department, and development of a more active intellectual community on campus—all for the benefit of both students and faculty.

Corporate faculty development programming can have some other important benefits. Such activities can often reach a large number of faculty even with a relatively small faculty development budget. They often touch faculty who are reluctant to pursue individual study or research. They can often have a direct impact on classroom teaching, especially when such activities are aimed at developing specific skills useful in the classroom, such as analyzing writing, listening, understanding statistics, using computers, and understanding specific new approaches to teaching and learning. Many faculty engaged in group activities have experienced a gain in self-confidence both in their scholarly pursuits and in their classroom teaching; for the college or university, such activities have meant an improvement in the community's intellectual life.

Third, curricular renewal and faculty renewal must be closely yet carefully interwoven. Curricular change is often a good way to encourage faculty development. However, for curriculum change to be implemented effectively, a great deal of preparation on the part of faculty is required. This means that faculty must be given time and support for teaching new content, providing new combinations in the curriculum, and developing new approaches.

Such preparatory experiences can be extremely enriching for faculty. In fact, people have said that curriculum change is often of greater benefit to faculty than it is to students. A number of institutions have devised new interdisciplinary courses in general education. Many of these courses have forced faculty members to learn about other disciplines, to teach alongside colleagues, and to explore new fields of thought with them. Faculty themselves are striving to integrate knowledge rather than leaving that role to the students.

However, if faculty development and curriculum development are not carefully interwoven, frustration can result. For example, on several campuses included in the AAC study, faculty were provided with special grants that enabled them to pursue study leaves in order to learn new disciplines. When they returned to campus, many were anxious to have an opportunity to develop interdisciplinary courses or to teach in the new, related field. Unfortunately, neither the curriculum committee nor the relevant departments were prepared to make the adaptations required to allow for these new approaches to teaching. Thus, both the faculty development program and faculty enthusiasm for teaching suffered. However, where faculty development opportunities have been closely linked with curriculum change, renewal of both curricular content and the teachers themselves has been promoted.

Fourth, teaching improvement programs can be successful if they are carried out with sensitivity. In the AAC project, the programs aimed at the improvement of teaching were usually the least successful on campus. Why was this so? Teaching is undoubtedly an extremely sensitive area for most faculty. As one faculty member remarked during the project, "Faculty are reluctant to think they can be told anything about teaching." Most programs aimed at the improvement of teaching suffered for two reasons: They were not specific enough, and they were too clinical in their approach.

Many teaching improvement programs were created around some general topic such as developing one's teaching skills. Most faculty were skeptical of such programs and stayed away. However, where the concentration was a specific skill improvement, such as on how to lead a discussion, how to use media resources, or how to handle problems in interdisciplinary teaching, faculty response was positive. Whenever faculty members felt that they could learn specific skills that would be useful in the classroom the very next day or over the next several months, they were ready to give the program a chance.

Often, teaching improvement programs have carried the suggestion that there was something clearly wrong with the teaching on campus. This clinical approach did not attract many patients. However, where the impression was given that all faculty have special talents and skills to share with one another, the response was quite positive.

Fifth, we must expand our ideas of scholarly professional development. Most people agree that there is a great deal of value in committing ideas to writing or in holding them out for public review in some way or another. Over the past two decades, a great deal of money and effort has gone into providing faculty with individual research grants aimed at publication and presentation of papers. At first glance, this seems to be a very positive situation. However, when one begins to probe, one finds that many faculty feel that scholarship is not being enhanced by existing faculty development programs. For example, younger faculty are being encouraged to publish very early in their career, often in very specialized areas. This is understandable, since working on the edge of a discipline in some specialized area is often the best way of getting published. One faculty member, himself a published scholar, became so concerned about this situation that he remarked: "Young faculty often publish too soon because of the pressure they feel. As a result, many good potential young scholars are being ruined." This situation has resulted in some real tension for younger faculty. At a time when they are trying to learn to teach in the broad, central areas of their discipline, they are forced to conduct research in narrow, marginal areas. The same situation has been troublesome for senior faculty as well. Many senior faculty are not publishing, as they feel that they will not or cannot compete for publication in national journals. However, they possess many valuable insights to contribute as a result of their years of teaching (Light, 1974).

Is the answer to this situation to stop researching, writing, and publishing? No, we need to develop new outlets for broader scholarship. Suggestions have included multiplying the opportunities for faculty to present papers on campus or in consortia. Various colleges could link together to enrich faculty through the exchange of manuscripts and the sharing of ideas. The hope is that more faculty would put their scholarly ideas into writing or at least to lay them out for public view in a meaningful way.

Sixth, while personnel management is not a strength of the academy, it is something that we must learn. In the world of business, a great deal of energy is spent on personnel management—evaluating people, providing regular feedback concerning these evaluations, giving encouragement and support for continuing development, correcting problem areas, and planning for long-term growth and development. Personnel management is not a strength of the academy. In fact, the very idea can be anathema to faculty members and administrators. At a recent faculty gathering at which the author addressed this subject, one faculty member objected strenuously to the use of the term management in relation to faculty matters. For the sake of such persons, we should perhaps substitute the term colleagueship and allow the same principles to apply. That is, for continuing faculty renewal, we need to give our colleagues feedback, support, and encouragement.

A good system of personnel management is crucial to faculty

development. We need to prepare department heads, deans, and others to link systems of evaluation and feedback with personal encouragement and rewards for continuing development. Some colleges have responded to this need by instituting training programs for department heads and appropriate administrators in order to promote better personnel management and faculty renewal throughout the institution.

Seventh, organizational change is usually necessary if faculty development is to become more prominent and permanent within an institution. Gardner (1965, p. 11) has written that "the development of abilities is at least in part a dialogue between the individual and his environment." Faculty and administrators must ask what kind of environment they are creating for faculty renewal on their campus. Are they creating a climate that is receptive to and demanding of faculty development?

In the author's travels to liberal arts colleges around the country, the most frequently mentioned factor by faculty as encouraging their continued renewal was the overall climate on campus. A positive climate for faculty renewal seemed to be encouraged by an adequate budget for faculty development activites; a committee structure that gave faculty development a prominent place, not a minor role; a reward structure that clearly encouraged continuing renewal; clear and demanding expectations for continuing renewal on the campus; and a community of support and encouragement from both faculty and administrators. In short, what made the most difference was a total campus environment which said that renewal of faculty was important and evidence that renewal would receive continuing support in a variety of concrete ways.

Creating and Developing Effective
Faculty Renewal Programs

During the last decade of experimentation in faculty development, we learned that how a college goes about its program development is as important as what it does to encourage renewal. In relation to the process for continuing faculty renewal, several items seem crucial: First, it is important for faculty to develop a sense of ownership of the renewal activities. Faculty must believe that the programs being initiated were primarily proposed by themselves in response to their own perceptions of their needs. Second, the purposes of the programs must be clear. In several instances, colleges failed to sort out their needs and purposes. In those cases, the programs faltered in relation to both planning and implementation. Third, administrators must be prepared to lead by bringing key faculty members together to encourage their colleagues' renewal. Administrators must also be prepared to move out of the way to allow for faculty ownership. Fourth, administrators must also make sure that programs are well managed. They should use a combination of representative faculty committees and careful overseeing of budgetary and funding guidelines to do so. Fifth, constant attention must be given to good communication of both the opportunities for faculty development and the results of renewal activities.

The most difficult question faced by colleges and universities in relation to faculty renewal in the years to come is this: How can effective programs be created or maintained during a time of scarce resources? Since the need is so great and since faculty development programs in most institutions are still in the relatively infant stage, another way to phrase the question is, How can we reach more faculty with fewer dollars during the coming decade?

Faculty development programs are often viewed as expensive items that should be reserved only for the most prestigious colleges and universities. Indeed, over the years, leading colleges and universities have put a great deal of money into programs of sabbatical leaves, travel to professional meetings, and research grants. It may well be that foundation and federal support during the 1970s encouraged them to do so, since many expensive programs were indeed made possible by outside funds. However, the past decade has also taught us that a wide variety of programs can be carried out with relatively small resources. This is true for both individual approaches and collective approaches to renewal.

To provide support for an individual faculty member's development often seems expensive, but it need not be. Even a relatively small grant ($400 to $500) for a specific project can have a profound effect upon a faculty member's teaching or scholarship. Such grants may allow for the purchase of books, resource materials, field research, travel to a research library, or assistance in manuscript development. More importantly, it can be a great psychological boost in that it shows that the faculty member's work in progress is worthy of encouragement and support. A number of colleges have had excellent results with a regular competitive program of small grants for faculty. Even sabbatical leave programs need not be expensive. When a department is large enough and when leaves are scheduled properly, a leave program, especially those of less than full pay, can actually save money for the institution. Other individual oriented programs have proven to be relatively low-cost as well—for example, faculty exchanges with other colleges, internships for faculty in nonacademic settings, and small grants for faculty to work with students in research projects.

More and more colleges are discovering that significant faculty development can occur at relatively low cost through corporate approaches to renewal. Every college has tremendous resources in its own faculty. Faculty members can teach one another through seminars, workshops, or even one-to-one teaching arrangements. Group approaches to faculty development are often quite cost-effective, as a large number of faculty can be included in the program at relatively low cost.

Faculty Development and Key Issues of the 1980s

For years, we in the academy have been warned that we would face times of tremendous difficulty and challenge in the 1980s. We were warned about enrollment difficulties, a significant drop in the number of students emerging from the high schools, a slumbering economy, continuing concerns about energy, and the accompanying problems of staff reductions and enrollment competition. Now, we are in the midst of such times. Institutions already have or soon will begin to retrench in staff. This retrenchment may mean that faculty development will be more important than ever. Many faculty will be called on to move into new related areas and to undergo retraining and renewal in the process. We will need to be flexible in our renewal programs to allow that retraining to take place, and we will need a sense of strong support, both for faculty who leave the institution and for faculty called on to assume new roles.

When campuses become smaller, faculty renewal programs can help to keep them active and lively. Smaller does not necessarily mean worse; in fact, it can even mean better. The faculty who stay may be in the same role or in a new teaching role. In either case, renewal programs can help them to be effective in relation to both curriculum content and new approaches to teaching.

Loss of Important Values in the 1980s? Colleges and universities are now in the midst of making adjustments to these times. Some institutions will do extremely well during the coming decade, others will struggle, while some will almost certainly fail. However, the most important question for the future of higher education may well be, Which values will emerge as the most prominent for American higher education in the next ten years? The transmission of values has always been an important role of higher education institutions. This role has been and will always be present, despite those who argue in favor of value-free education. Total objectivity is impossible—within the classroom or outside it. Values are constantly taught, not only by teachers but also by those who administer and by those who set policies, whether through faculty and administrative committees, boards of regents, or state legislatures.

Thus, the problems that we face in the future will not be a lack of values. Rather, the question is, Which values will we teach, both inside and outside the classroom? Which values will we promote, and which values will we discourage through our commitment to and structuring of faculty development programs?

Traditionally, the academy has stressed the values of quality, community, cooperation, institutional loyalty, intellectual and moral leadership, which grew out of its concern for solid scholarship, scientific inquiry, human development, humanistic education, and service. Faith in these traditional values now appears to be eroding for two basic reasons: the confusion about mission and the emphasis on expediency in our institutions.

Institutions of higher education appear to be increasingly ambivalent about the values for which they stand. Even during the growth era of higher education, many institutions failed to sort out their missions. There was little need to do so, as long as students continued to arrive on campus. Now, as student enrollment declines, many institutions are scrambling to find new markets and to install new programs with little attention to their central mission.

The old values, which related primarily to the search for truth and service to humanity, are increasingly being replaced by values dictated by economic considerations. Values that once seemed to be very important for the central mission of an educational institution have often been lost sight of in the cost-benefit equations. Education has always been concerned with the practical. In the past, however, *practical* referred to what was useful to the good or well-being of mankind. Now, *practical* is understood as expedient—what might help bring more students or more funds to the institution, at least for the moment.

It is ironic that this confusion of values in our institutions of higher education comes at a time when values questions are receiving increasing attention in the curriculum. Throughout the past decade, the emphasis on the teaching of values and ethics has increased. Yet, at the same time institutions seem to be giving little attention to the values that they teach and promote through administrative and policy-making practices and through faculty development programs.

During the coming decade, what values that we have stood for in the past are we in danger of losing? Five values—quality, community, cooperation, institutional loyalty, and intellectual and moral leadership—will be crucial in the coming years. These values are in danger of being lost, or severely eroded, or—worse yet—completely ignored during this period of constraint.

Quality. Colleges and universities of every kind and size have traditionally held high the value of quality. My focus here is not on the older, elitist view of quality, which assigned quality to only institutions that took in outstanding students and that therefore turned out outstanding students. The real mark of excellence for an educational institution in the years to come will be what it does to improve the intellectual and moral qualities of students—and, where the institution's particular mission calls for it, the spiritual, physical, and social maturity of students as well. However, if our institutions are to have a quality impact on students, the students recruited must match both the mission of the institution and the resources available on campus. If an institution in its scramble for new students or new market areas seeks to attract inappropriate groups of students and then fails to provide resources on campus to promote student growth, including proper preparation and development for faculty, and if it has a high rate of attrition as a result, quality is clearly lost in the process.

Community. In many institutions, we may have passed the point at which we could talk about maintaining community in the sense of a group of persons dedicated to a common goal and strongly supportive of one another in that dedication. Still, certain qualities associated with community, such as collegiality, participation, communication, fairness, and trust, must not be lost. During interviews in the AAC project in faculty development, I was distressed to find that many of the traditional values associated with community were no longer given the proper attention, even on relatively small campuses. In many interviews, faculty members spoke of their loneliness and of the lack of support. They felt estranged from other faculty because it was hard to relate to persons outside the discipline or subdiscipline, because communication between departments or divisions was poor, because they felt that they had little support from colleagues or administrators for their particular interest, or because they felt that they did not participate enough in the decision making on campus, which in turn raised questions of the fairness of decisions and of the ability to place trust in the process.

As a result of the shift away from community-building processes, our old sense of collegiality and community seems to have been replaced by a legalistic system of operating. This process is reflected in the enlargement of faculty and staff handbooks over the past decade. It is extremely difficult to find a sense of community when we operate through an increasingly legalistic system of relationships within the academy.

Cooperation. American colleges and universities often stress the concepts of liberality, tolerance, and the value of consensus in their curriculum. Our administrative and governance practices seem now to be abandoning these values in favor of hard-line positions, intolerance, lack of understanding, and often a lack of forgiveness. At one institution, during a debate at a faculty meeting about including a new program in the curriculum, a group of faculty in the humanities division responded by walking out. Many of these faculty returned to the classroom the next day to teach some of the great lessons of history and literature concerning liberality and tolerance. As with community, the sense of cooperation can only be fostered on a campus where both administrative and faculty leaders are committed to its importance.

Institutional Loyalty. In recent years, faculty and even administrators have seemed to give more loyalty to their particular profession than to the place where they work. Faculty think of themselves first as biologists, political scientists, or sociologists and only second as a member of a particular faculty. Of course, serving one's profession in this narrow sense has benefits both for the individual and for higher education in general, but service to one's particular disciplinary profession must be balanced by service to one's college and community.

Intellectual and Moral Leadership. One of the most important roles of our educational institutions in the past has been their independent critical view of other institutions within our society. Both faculty and administrators have served as sensitive critics and evaluators of the goals and directions of business, government, the church, and other agencies. In this role, they have advocated a continuing search for truth, and they have constantly raised the important moral and ethical questions. There is a great danger that colleges and universities will allow financial problems, internal battles, and the search for money and students to get in the way of this important function during the 1980s.

Values in Relation to Faculty Development. What are the implications of this potential loss of values for faculty development programs? For each of the five value areas just cited, both the content and structure of faculty development programs can make a significant difference.

Quality. There will be tremendous pressure in the years ahead to abandon faculty development programs and funding altogether. Yet, quality cannot be maintained without a constant sense of renewal by individuals, by groups, and by the institution as a whole. Faculty development funding and programs must be seen as extremely important for our institutions, both for the short term and for the long run. As one college president stressed, "Faculty development funds are the most cost-effective dollars we have." Only this type of positive, committed attitude to faculty renewal can ensure that the quality of our efforts to serve the various types of students in our educational institutions will remain high.

Community. Faculty development programs can either enhance the faculty's sense of community or detract from it. If faculty have a sense of ownership in their own renewal and if this sense is backed by administrative support, other faculty will be willing to join in the process. Also, if faculty development programs are created to give opportunities for both individual and corporate renewal, some of the tendencies toward isolationism and compartmentalism within our institutions can be countered. Faculty can be brought together for their own renewal and for the development of a vital intellectual community.

Cooperation. When faculty development programs are structured in a multifaceted, flexible way and when the versatility of faculty is taken into account, a sense of cooperation can be fostered. Where good programs of faculty evaluation are linked with effective renewal programs, faculty can have a stronger sense of cooperating with one another, of listening to one another, and of giving support to one another in their renewal efforts. Also, faculty can learn to work together through consortium arrangements, through departmental programming, through interdisciplinary efforts, and through campuswide development activities in a spirit of cooperation. This cooperative spirit can increase the involvement of faculty members in their own renewal, and it can help to establish the proper climate for both students and faculty as they seek to learn from others around them.

Institutional Loyalty. A strong faculty development program can have a very positive impact on the renewal of faculty loyalty not only to their disciplines but to the institution as a whole. When the institution has a clear sense of mission, when it has demonstrated a sense of concern for the faculty member's life and career even in a time of retrenchment, and when it has shown its dedication to individual and collective growth and renewal, the responses of faculty can be very positive toward the institution, even in—perhaps especially in—times of difficulty.

Intellectual and Moral Leadership. Faculty development programs must focus on key intellectual and moral questions of our time. There will be pressure in the coming years to avoid controversial issues and to support faculty in their renewal efforts only in areas that seem to meet shifts in student enrollment or to promote new markets. If faculty development programs ignore the great questions of biomedical discoveries, socioethical issues, political concerns, and other deep ethical questions, the public will feel in the long run that our institutions have lost their integrity. Perhaps more important, faculty will not participate in development programs that seem not to support their own sense of integrity and search for truth.

Creating an Atmosphere for Renewing Faculty Resources

As expressed earlier, the most important thing that we can do in the years to come is to create a climate on campus that promotes continuing renewal of our most important resource, faculty. We can do so by providing adequate budgets, by making our expectations clear, and by providing support and reward across campus. Still, many fear that none of these steps will be effective in countering the despair and low morale that difficult times can create (Wheeler, 1978). Nevertheless, the years to come do not have to mean malaise and discouragement. While it is clearly possible to view the years ahead as difficult or even as the worst of times, it some ways they may turn out to be the best of times.

Those involved in marriage counseling have discovered time and time again that, when a couple faces a period of crisis, one of two things can happen. If the couple cannot stand the pressures, they drift apart, blame each other for their problems, and finally separate and divorce. However, the time of crisis can also bring them closer together. They examine their commitments, goals, and concerns, and as a result they become a stronger, more mature, more loving couple.

It is possible for us in higher education to go in either direction. During the years to come, we could lose our sense of concern for our important traditional values, fight nonproductively for a declining student pool, and lose our sense of direction and integrity and our continuing sense of renewal. However, all the pressures that we face can also force us to examine our purposes and direction carefully, to renew our commitment to important values, and to help us see the need for constant renewal. In fact, these times may force us to do what we should have been doing all along — dedicating ourselves to the continuing renewal of our most important resource.

References

Astin A. W. *Four Critical Years: Effects of College on Beliefs, Attitudes, and Knowledge.* San Francisco: Jossey-Bass, 1977.

Bergquist, W. H., and Phillips, S. R. *A Handbook for Faculty Development.* Vol. I, Washington: Council for the Advancement of Small Colleges, 1975. Vol. II, 1977, Vol. III, 1981.

Chickering, A. W. *Education and Identity.* San Francisco: Jossey-Bass, 1969.

Centra, J. A. *Faculty Development Practices in U.S. Colleges and Universities.* Princeton: Educational Testing Service, 1976.

Freedman, M. (Ed.). *Facilitating Faculty Development.* New Directions in Higher Education, no. 1. San Francisco: Jossey-Bass, 1973.

Gaff, J. G. (Ed.). *Institutional Renewal Through the Improvement of Teaching.* New Directions in Higher Education, no. 24. San Francisco: Jossey-Bass, 1978.

Gaff, J. G. *Toward Faculty Renewal: Advances in Faculty, Instructional and Organizational Development.* San Francisco: Jossey-Bass, 1975.

Gardner, J. *Self-Renewal: The Individual and the Innovative Society.* New York: Harper, 1965.

Heath, D. *Growing Up in College.* San Francisco: Jossey-Bass, 1968.

Katz, J., and Associates. *No Time for Youth: Growth and Constraint in College Students.* San Francisco: Jossey-Bass, 1968.

Levinson, D. *The Seasons of a Man's Life.* New York: Knopf, 1978.

Light, D. "Thinking About Faculty." *Daedalus,* 1974, *103,* 258–264.

Nelsen, W. C. "Faculty Development: Prospects and Potential for the 1980s." *Liberal Education,* 1979, *65,* 141–149.

Nelsen, W. C. *Renewal of the Teacher-Scholar.* Washington, D.C.: Association of American Colleges, 1981.

Nelsen, W. C., and Siegel, M. E. (Eds.). *Effective Approaches to Faculty Development.* Washington D.C.: Association of American Colleges, 1980.

Perry, W. G., Jr. *Forms of Intellectural and Ethical Development in the College Years.* New York: Holt, Rinehart and Winston, 1968.

Sheehy, G. *Passages.* New York: Dutton, 1974.

Wheeler, B. M. "Hope and Despair in the Academy." *The Chronicle of Higher Education,* May 15, 1978, p. 48.

William C. Nelsen is president of Augustana College in Sioux Falls, South Dakota. He served as director of the Association of American Colleges' recent project on faculty development, which was funded by the Andrew W. Mellon Foundation.

Careful analysis demonstrates the overall failure of faculty development programs to become a permanent fixture in the organizational structure of colleges and universities.

Faculty Development: The Institutional Side

William Toombs

A rich variety of endeavors appeared under the generous banner of faculty development in the late 1960s and 1970s. Resourceful, perceptive people tried to work through puzzling problems with great energy in new ways. The trail began with instructional improvement. The first efforts were concentrated on presentation techniques, often those involving audiovisual and other technical support. Then, attention shifted to teachers' interaction with learners and students' reactions. Later concerns about instructional strategies and learning styles were raised. At the same time came an emphasis on organizational development. Most recently, the development of individual careers has emerged as a major concern. Moreover, a strain of evaluation runs through all faculty development efforts.

These different lines of interest are clearly recorded by research reports and general summaries in the literature. Gaff (1975) provides both a running account and a continuous dialogue on various dimensions of faculty development. Bergquist and Phillips (1975, 1977) describe some useful applications of various development ideas. Stordahl (1981) presents a good summary of the main features of the faculty development movement. There can be little doubt that many discov-

R. G. Baldwin and R. T. Blackburn (Eds.). *College Faculty: Versatile Human Resources in a Period of Constraint.*
New Directions for Institutional Research, no. 40. San Francisco: Jossey-Bass, December 1983.

eries turned up along this well-marked trail will find a modest but permanent place in the role structure of alert academics — on student evaluation of courses, for example. Also, some aspects of faculty development, such as instructional improvement, have fared better in two-year colleges than they have in four-year settings, while others, such as professional development, have prospered better in liberal arts colleges than elsewhere.

Centra (1978) analyzed practices as they existed at the high point of the faculty development movement. In the 1975–76 academic year, more than 60 percent of the institutions surveyed could identify some faculty development practices, and 44 percent had an office or a person engaged in such activity. By the early 1980s, the scene had changed, and a survey of instructional improvement centers by Gustafson and Bratton (1983) found that many units had disappeared. In a sample of seventy-two centers, twenty (28 percent) had closed, and more than half of the remainder reported budget cuts.

An Assessment and Some Questions

As a series of trials in a new arena, faculty development programs have made some contributions. However, viewed from the broad sweep of institutional operations, the overall assessment is that faculty development has had very little impact on institutions. It has commanded insufficient resources to find a place in the budget. Moreover, faculty development has no natural or correct location in the formal organization of institutions. In operational terms, faculty development programs do not carry weight in the processes of appointment, promotion, and tenure. Finally, they are not an indispensable component of the academic role, either at the entry level or at the advanced level.

Why should this be so? What accounts for the low impact of faculty development programs after more than a decade of thoughtful trials? Is it possible that other approaches could yield stronger results? The questions are more important than the conclusions, because one knows intuitively and logically that the substance of what has been labeled *faculty development* matters to the profession. Every major profession has accepted the idea of continuing professional education in some form. Is the professoriate to be different?

The rapid evolution of knowledge and the special importance of new knowledge carry a mandate for professional updating. The matriculation of students who represent ever broader bands of the socioeconomic spectrum and the intellectual scale also requires increased understanding of the learning process among those who guide it. Ties between the academic world and society, particularly the economic sector, present problems of curriculum design and course emphasis that were not encountered until very recently. In short, the need for a rational foundation for faculty development programs is obvious.

Explanations for the low institutional impact of such programs may reside in the program elements of faculty development efforts, in something within the institution, or in both. There is already a good deal of introspective analysis by those who were closely associated with the organized efforts of the past ten years. Less attention has been devoted to the environment in which they sought to establish these programs. Consequently, I will examine this aspect of the institutional side in this chapter. My point is that, as social institutions faced with massive change, colleges and universities adopted a conservative posture, which is embodied in the notion of the managed institution. The limitations of the managed institution concept are concentrated in a set of personnel premises and practices opposed to the human resources view of faculty development. I will outline an alternative personnel policy that can encourage the institutionalization of professional development. The notion of institutionalization, which is common to sociology and anthropology, will provide the main thread for my description.

Living with an Institution

The rudimentary social wisdom behind the creation of institutional forms is that some activities of the mind, body, and spirit are so important that they must be established and preserved against change. There are several avenues toward such regularization. All are generally used in concert to achieve social control. There is always an elite, whose role is carefully prescribed and maintained by the elect. If, for example, every faculty member were expected to exhibit many of the forty-five behaviors noted by Centra (1978), then we could say that faculty development had been institutionalized around the academic role.

There is also a tendency to make a special place in the organizational structure for vital activities. The attempts to create educational development officers and centers of faculty development illustrate this approach to institutionalization. Then, too, the necessary activity can be made part of the regular functioning of the institution. In these cases, it becomes normal business routine.

Again, efforts to place faculty development on the agenda of academic committees have not been fruitful. Finally, every social organization has a value system that weighs and binds role, structure, and function to give each its relative worth and importance. Participation in faculty development is not highly valued.

The intention behind this pattern of interrelated behaviors is to ensure the social institutions against change. But, change they do, quietly and often secretly in the more orderly societies, violently in the more volatile settings. Changes in size, scope, and nature of services are particularly difficult for social institutions and their responsible members to handle. Faced with incomprehensible or untraditional conditions, social institutions tend to adopt a conservative posture reaching back to their central core of values and behavior and rejecting the new or marginal ideas.

Higher education is an institution, and, as Kerr (1982) has observed, its attributes are eternal. However, this institution has confronted changes of greater magnitude and scope than the other institutions of our society during the last twenty years. The struggle to comprehend and accept change coming from outside the institution has blocked and diverted much of the innovative change within institutions.

Recording Evolution

The customary way of perceiving and analyzing the general phenomenon of change in higher education is by periodic updates. Usually, an individual scholar catalogues the emergent features and presents us with a replacement paradigm (Kuhn, 1970), to enhance reorientation. Bronowski (1973, p. 24) puts it eloquently: "Each culture tries to fix its visionary moment, when it was transformed by a new conception either of nature or of man."

Wilhelm von Humboldt fixed such a moment in his memoranda for the University of Berlin in 1910, which catapulted that university into the scientific era (Humboldt, 1970). Humboldt knew that he was dealing with institutional change: "The idea of disciplined intellectual activity, embodied in institutions, is the most valuable element in the moral culture of the nation. These intellectual institutions have as their task the cultivation of science and scholarship in the deepest and broadest sense" (p. 242). Later, he makes the case for the central emphasis of the scientific university by stating: "If, however, the principal of cultivating science and scholarship for their own sake is placed in a dominant position . . . other matters may be disregarded. Neither unity nor full-roundedness will be lacking; each naturally fosters the other and a proper balance will thereby by maintained. This is the secret of good research method" (p. 245).

Flexner (in Kerr, 1963, p. 6) identified the transformations of his time, summarizing the university as "an organism characterized by highness and definiteness of aim, unity of spirit, and purpose." Kerr caught the sense of the postwar university in its American expression. He described the university as a pluralistic organization — a "multiversity" — made up of many distinct parts, each of them capable of the high aims, unified spirit, and purpose that once characterized the whole of Flexner's university.

We understand intuitively that these landmark reconceptualizations consolidate a process of continuous evolutionary change. Bronowski (1973, p. 59) calls attention to a feature of cultural evolution that is significant for this analysis: "Inventions may be rare, but they spread fast through a culture." When rapid diffusion is combined with external changes of great magnitude — exactly the case in higher education in the last twenty years — then social institutions must confront especially trying conditions.

The Tide of Transformation

The size of the enterprise has increased in every dimension, and a comparison with other institutions — health and justice systems, for example — make this clear. The structure of the institution has altered. The mission has been amended in unusual, even strange, ways. Lines of guidance from society at large are more difficult to interpret. From a sociological point of view, these add up to a massive institutional transformation.

Looking first at the simple dimension of size and using the last thirty years as the critical period, what do we find? The number of practicing lawyers has increased by a factor of 2.1. However, faculty at colleges and universities have increased 3.4 times to the point where there are now about twice as many academics as there are practitioners in the next largest profession. In terms of the number of colleges and universities increased from 1,863 in 1950 to 3,231 in 1980, a factor of 1.7. In contrast, the number of hospitals increased only slightly — from 6,788 institutions to 6,965.

The structure has altered as well. The creation of 1,200 community colleges, the transformation of teachers' colleges into comprehensive public universities, and the shift in the ratio of public to private colleges signify the arrival of a complex and distinctive system. The tendency to replace the term higher education with the term postsecondary education symbolizes this change in scope.

A different set of conditions faces higher education in other, qualitative ways. For as many as forty years, the directions for colleges and universities were bound up with national trends and with trends in other social institutions. Neither choice nor separate justification for the academy was required. Science and technology created an endless frontier for manpower trained at increasingly higher levels. Shortages in the professions generated by rising populations sustained the expansion of teaching and new preprofessional programs. Research capacity, particularly at the basic levels, was in short supply in both industry and the public sector. Sponsored academic research grew in response. The numbers of young people in the population gave political salience to funding measures in state and national legislatures. What higher education should be doing was so clear that interpretation was all but unnecessary. But, since 1975, these trends have disintegrated, differentiated by region, field of study, and industry. As if to confirm this end of trends, the withdrawal of federal initiatives with funding to match has removed the guidance of public policy. Institutional missions and institutional directions are now a matter of choice, and independent decision adds another task to the consequences of institutional change.

The Response: Managed Institutions

The weight of these institutional transformations has come to rest on those in positions of leadership in academic administration and on the maintenance system that usually functions unobtrusively in a stable social institution. The struggle to comprehend the meaning of all this change has occupied the academy for about fifteen years and preempted both experimentation and innovation. Indeed, as Harold Enarson, former president of Ohio State, once remarked, the essence of the university has eluded both her friends and her enemies.

The struggle first to understand the institution in its new form, then to find an appropriate direction, has taken a single path. Attention has been fixed almost myopically on the corporate tradition — the image of the college or university as a managed enterprise not altogether unlike a business organization. The more diffuse, comfortable melange of collegium, convocation, or federalism symbolized by the term republic of scholars was contained by the new notion of governance. The welfare and survival of the institution, not of its individual inhabitants or of its components, became the primary unit of action and attention. Such emphasis on the managed entity, on the whole rather than the parts, looked toward a college or university with just the right rank distribution, the ideal tenure ratio, departments of manageable size, standard program codes, and cost centers, all bound together by an effective budget and orchestrated by a continuous planning function.

Under this view of the college or university, effectiveness is manifest in the fiscal condition of the whole enterprise, not in the educational or intellectual strength of its components. It is assumed, of course, that well-managed institutions produce good educational programs, but there is little evidence that relates the two. To keep this formal rigidity within the bounds of reality, more relaxed theories of organization have begun to appear. The academic world has found congenial recent ideas of organized anarchies, loosely coupled systems, and contingency theory.

Nevertheless, whatever the benefits of this managed institution approach may be, it is not the best climate for thinking about and experimenting with the development of human resources. The abilities of individuals take their value from the way they can serve the requirements of the institution's management objectives. Personnel, an expensive commodity in the budgetary equation, must perforce be adjusted to fit the master plan of the sound institution. Faculty development was moving in quite the opposite direction, away from an instrumental view of individuals and toward the cultivation of intrinsic abilities, wherever they might lead. The early emphasis of faculty development programs on improving instructional technique gave way to a concern for career and life development. In retrospect, it seems clear that faculty development was swimming against the tide. It could not succeed.

Of course, the managed institution approach did help academic leadership to confront the massive social forces at work on the social institution of higher education and on the component institutions of higher education. But, there were costs. One has already been noted—the downgrading of human resources to an instrumental factor. I will return to this topic later. Other areas, too, were ignored and as a result escaped the range of university influence. The rapid and extensive growth of executive, professional, and technical training programs in noneducational settings came about because higher education was so preoccupied with its management problems, that it could not see the importance of these educational challenges except where they fitted into older conventions (Black, 1979). In a similar way, a wide range of new organizational forms for research and development appeared to take over what was once a major domain of academic research. Again, the flexibility of the managed institution foreclosed one whole set of options. While the focus of this chapter is on faculty development, we must also note that other kinds of development met the same obstacles.

The Obstacle to Institutionalization

In the managed institution, the principal obstacle to the institutionalization of faculty development resides in the premises and practices of pesonnel policy. Only if they are altered can a path for the human resource approach to professional development by cleared.

The personnel policies of most four-year institutions are rooted in the years just after World War II, when enrollments were rising and there were general shortages of faculty in all categories. With talent in short supply, the pattern of benefits, career path assumptions, recognitions, and rewards was premised on scarcity. The only suitable approach was to attract people to the institution and design personnel practices to place the weight of reward on staying there. Of course, there was a belief probation period, but in the whole the concept was that of a closed system with a lifetime career ladder possible inside the institution. Retirement plans took a long time before holdings were vested — ten years — and the good payoffs were reserved for thirty-year veterans. Health benefits offered few options, but costs were kept low. Tuition benefits for children (and, in the private sector, even if they attended other institutions) were widely used as an incentive to stay. The career track for faculty was seen as a lifetime commitment to the field. Professional development was to be handled by the individual through foundation or government grants. Leaves followed the sabbatical pattern, whether it fitted conditions or not. A move into an administrative post was seen as a point of no return, and people seldom made it. The archetypal individual in this scheme was a young male with a wife and a growing family at home. The underlying objective was to create as stable a personnel system as possible for the faculty, thereby insulating the institution against unmanageable change.

This was not a bad system for the times. Now, however, events have overtaken both the premises and the practices to create a new set of requirements that they often serve poorly. Naturally, there has been a great deal of effort to introduce practices that will remedy one ill or another without compromising the premise. For example, the TIAA–CREF plans permit career change to another academic institution. However, they do not provide a transition to the nonacademic world without penalty. Early retirement options and "buy-outs" allow institutions to get relief from the scarcity-based system without changing the premise. Part-time faculty, contract appointments, and other nontenure track arrangements have the similar effect of preserving a shrinking system without changing the premise.

The Shape of Alternatives

What would a set of personnel premises and practices look like if it were based on conditions today—which it seems, will be with us for the next two generations? Based not on scarcity but on an abundance of talent, the objective would be to achieve a dynamic flow of ability through the institution. Programs of human resource development would bring short-term benefits while people were in the academic world and follow them to other settings if they left. The motivation would arise from personal and professional advancement, not from the weaker stimulus of service to the organization. In this context, the whole range of activities developed under the egis of faculty development would make sense.

Can the realities of practical policies be fitted into the premises of abundant talent? Many of the components are already present in other professions and businesses. "Cafeteria" packages of retirement and health benefits would allow people to meet not only their needs but their choices more effectively. Two married professionals could factor plans for advanced study, childbearing, or career change into their lives. More flexibility in the early years could be traded off against smaller benefits in later retirement options. Mixed contracts—similar in form to the medical service contract commonly used in medical schools—would accommodate a much richer mix of research, teaching, and service to business or industry. Articulation agreements that make it possible for faculty to teach or conduct research on a time-shared basis across departments are already in place at some institutions.

Of course, personnel planning under this flow concept would be different. Rather than focusing on individuals, planning would for the most part concentrate on necessary slots largely determned by program design. These slots could be filled in a variety of ways that would reflect different contracts, persons at different career stages, and even professors from other departments. Only at the most advanced levels of undergraduate and graduate study would planning be based on incumbent, established faculty members.

In such a setting, most of the elements of faculty development would take on new meaning. The motivation would be individual development. Instructional improvement would become a matter of improving technique, not a confession of inadequacy. Career development would begin early, it would deal with matters of substance, and it would permit the construction of real alternatives. The institution would reap the immediate benefits that come with every human resource approach: better motivation, enthusiasm for work, involvement in the issues of each day, and a heightened sense of learning. In the long run, those who left the institution would enhance its reputation and carry with them the quality of active imagination that Alfred North Whitehead saw as a major component of education.

References

Bergquist, W. H., and Phillips, S. R. *Handbook for Faculty Development.* Vol. I, Vol. II. Washington, D.C.: Council for the Advancement of Small Colleges, 1975, 1977.

Black, G. J. *Trends in Management Development and Education.* White Plains, N.Y.: Knowledge Industry Publications, 1979.

Bronowski, J. *Ascent of Man.* New York: Little, Brown, 1973.

Centra, J. A. "Types of Faculty Development Programs." *Journal of Higher Education,* 1978, *49* (2), 151–161.

Flexner, A. *Universities: American, English, German.* New York: Oxford University Press, 1930.

Gaff, J. G. *Toward Faculty Renewal.* San Francisco: Jossey-Bass, 1975.

Gustafson, K. L., and Bratton, B. "Institutional Improvement Centers in Higher Education: A Status Survey." Paper presented at the annaul meeting of The American Educational Research Association, Montreal, 1983.

Humboldt, W. von. "Uber die innere and äussere Organisaton des höheren wissenschaft lichen Anstalten zu Berlin." ("On the Spirit and Organizational Framework of Intellectual Institutions in Berlin.") Edward Shil's translation, *Minerva,* April 1970, pp. 242–250.

Kerr, C. *The Uses of the University.* Cambridge, Mass.: Harvard University Press, 1963.

Kerr, C. "Uses of the University Two Decades Later: Postscript 1982." *Change,* 1982, *14,* 23–31.

Kuhn, T. S. *The Structure of Scientific Revolutions.* (2nd ed.) Chicago: University of Chicago Press, 1970.

Stordahl, B. "Faculty Development: A Survey of Literature of the Seventies." *Research Currents* in the *AAHE Bulletin,* 1981, *33* (7), 7–10.

William Toombs is director of the Center for the Study of Higher Education, Pennsylvania State University, College Park. His research has focused on faculty and curriculum.

This chapter pursues some implications of the issues discussed
by the authors of the preceding chapters. Attention is focused
on Chapter Seven, since Toombs argues that the movement has
not realized its potential.

Concluding Comments

Robert T. Blackburn
Roger G. Baldwin

The authors of the preceding chapters have laid out the problems, directed the reader to the best sources of information, described a variety of strategies, and detailed the kinds of information that an institution needs in order to maintain and best to achieve its personnel and institutional goals. In this chapter, we will comment on some of the issues that the authors have raised, and we will conclude with a discussion of the implications.

In Chapter Three, Lee rightfully calls our attention to the hazards of forecasting the future. One needs to go back only a few years and read what the pundits were saying then about today. The late Allan Cartter (1976), the best student of faculty supply and demand, was off by 33 percent in his 1975 forecast of the number of Ph.D.'s who would be graduating in 1980, although he had accurate enrollment data and he was projecting only five years ahead. Our guesses about the state of the economy in 1995 — the year when the number of current faculty who will reach age sixty-five will accelerate rapidly — are hazardous at best. We will only be lucky if they turn out to be right. We simply cannot know what kinds of decisions faculty and institutions will make tomorrow.

R. G. Baldwin and R. T. Blackburn (Eds.). *College Faculty: Versatile Human Resources in a Period of Constraint.*
New Directions for Institutional Research, no. 40. San Francisco: Jossey-Bass, December 1983.

Nonetheless, some critical issues require action today. To employ the dominant economic and industrial metaphors of the current literature on postsecondary education, the higher education enterprise is distinctive in that it is the exclusive producer of its own employees. In addition, the production process is a lengthy one. For example, the average elapsed time between the B.A. and the Ph.D. in the humanities is more than ten years. Said another way, the assistant professor of philosophy whom we need in 1995 will have been an entering graduate in 1981. Our production line is spreading over a long period of time. It is not surprising that we are frequently out of phase with need. Right now, we are graduating thousands in the humanities although academic positions in those fields are virtually nonexistent. Furthermore, we will continue to do so for the next decade. Indeed, there will be a lost generation of humanists, at least as far as formal higher education is concerned, unless alternative strategies are introduced to take in new graduates.

Some believe that there will not be a faculty shortage beginning in 1995 simply because of the oversupply of students now in graduate school. Those already in the pipeline will continue to trickle out. This approach to future college and university staffing is analagous to the sperm bank solution to the need for future human creativity but to us it seems spurious. One does not put brains in a deep freeze and thaw them out when they are needed at some later date. The graduate of today or tomorrow who does not begin a scholarly career and maintain it will have no value a dozen years from now. Colleges and universities will want the newly minted potential scholar, not the untried and untested relic — and rightfully so.

Thus, we are facing a very serious problem today. The number of students entering graduate study, especially in the humanities, is dropping appreciably. Furthermore, as the recent Princeton (Bowen, 1981) and Chicago (University of Chicago Record, 1982) reports document all too dramatically, there is a real decline in the ability level of those who do enter graduate study. Consequently, both the future supply of faculty and the continuous production of knowledge are threatened. This critical issue is clearly a collective one for higher education, which no single institution is capable of solving. At the same time, every institution must contribute in its own way to the solution.

In Chapter Four, Patton raises another set of staffing issues as he addresses tactics and strategies that can increase the leaving rate. To begin with, as already noted, colleges and universities are different kinds of workplaces, and they are staffed by different kinds of people than almost all other kinds of human organizations. Instead of the complete separation given to a retiree at, say, Ford Motor Company — whether the person is an engineer, an assembly line worker, an economist, or an executive — a college confers emeritus status on its faculty. They may teach from time to time, have an office, take part in social and political events, serve on doctoral committees, obtain grants, and write. In fact, some emeritus faculty hardly change their life-style. Of course, some pack up and in essence sever almost all their connections with the institution. That is also a faculty option. In any case, retirement is much less a psychological adjustment problem for academics than it is for other kinds of professionals.

A second aspect of this phenomenon needs to be taken into account before we can draw the implications. As we learn about adult development and critical life stages, it is becoming evident that faculty also deal differently with the mortality syndrome — the recognition that there is less of my life left than I have already lived, that I have only a certain number of years left in which to accomplish the tasks and goals that I have set for myself. Levinson and others (1978) fix a definitive time for this troublesome period. The certain number of years left is usually the number of years remaining until age sixty-five, the traditional age for retirement. But, faculty realize that they can keep on working for the rest of their lives. For faculty, age fifty-five is not the crisis that it is for others.

A possible consequence of workplace compatibility and the opportunity to resolve mental health type problems is that faculty will question early retirement, even retirement at age sixty-five or seventy. The potential problem is further complicated by the changes in equity for women and retirement accounts, and it could become even more complex as a result of lawsuits prompted by seemingly unequal individually negotiated settlements. That is, when one "undesirable" gets special benefits to quit and another gets different benefits to leave, somebody will eventually want all the benefits that both have received.

As a result, colleges and universities may have to become even more creative in their personnel policies than they already have been. Increased use of part-time faculty is already evident. However, this employment practice is used more to give institutions budgetary flexibility than it is to accomplish organizational or personal goals. What is most needed is options for the later career years. Faculty could reduce their work load, with the assurance of support services — research or clerical assistance, for example — continuing beyond official retirement. More people will have to be hired who see moving out as a legitimate phase in one's life. The one life — one career protestant work ethic is questioned by Sarason (1977). There can be no doubt that it is time for colleges and universities to examine the implications of the work ethic, too. These organizations have appreciable grounds on which to create alternative models. Both faculty and administrators are imaginative entrepreneurs. The time is ripe for some innovations in the conditions of work within academe.

Both McKeachie and Nelsen deal with the faculty who remain, many of whom need assistance if they are to be renewed and to continue to grow and develop, therefore achieving their goals and those of the institution. McKeachie's review of the literature on the biology, psychology, and sociology of aging in this country makes clear what is and is not possible. We learn that within the psychological domain, the deterioration of mental ability is not a problem for those who continue to exercise these capacities.

In many ways the sociological literature on aging is more disturbing, although, on the surface, attitudes about the importance of chronological age seem easier to alter than the decline of one's mental capacities. We live in a society that stereotypes negatively. Even if college faculty work together across age strata and in collegial and supportive ways, institutional influence is still tipped toward senior faculty and divisions do occur. Young faculty feel increased tensions today because their career fates often lie in the hands of older professors. It is understandable that stereotypical remarks and actions will result even by those who know better.

Society has made some progress over the past two decades in recognizing cultural and ethnic differences and in the tolerance of persons and groups different from the mainstream. Academics will have to heed their own behavior within the workplace if faculty renewal is to take place. As McKeachie has pointed out, repetitive patterns too easily become fixed. Diversity and challenge for older faculty decline and the stereotypes of aging can become self-fulfilling. At the same time, higher educational organizations have the greatest potential for breaking down barriers to continuous growth.

Nelsen has learned what works well, and in Chapter Six he describes the basic ingredients of successful programs. We do not know what is the current state of health of various faculty development initiatives or even if there is a positive relationship between better programs and longevity. That one can accomplish both institutional and personal goals by such a simple and straightforward activity as revising the curriculum — for example by establishing interdisciplinary courses — provides hope that not all will be lost for those whose only career is in the academic world.

Toombs's persuasive analysis in Chapter Seven is provocative and more—it is devastating. Among other things, Toombs says that the leading experts on the institutionalization of innovations are blind on their own turf. (This would not be the first time that universities failed to use their own resources to solve their own problems.) Of course, we can examine Toombs's argument in several different ways. One way is simply to demonstrate that he is wrong. For example, another explanation for the failure of faculty development programs to be institutionalized is that they have not been needed. Teaching was never as bad as the loud voices of the late 1960s claimed. Student rating scores have always been high. At the University of Michigan, for example, more than 90 percent of the faculty receive overall teaching performance scores above four on a five-point scale (McKeachie, 1983). In a study of faculty in liberal arts colleges, O'Connell (1979) learned that faculty who did not participate in faculty development programs were just as active in revising their courses as faculty who did.

In a similar manner, one could argue that faculty know how to continue to learn and that they do learn. The needed resources are at hand—the library as well as colleague scholars with whom to share ideas and from whom to receive instruction and constructive criticism. All the things that faculty need in order to continue to grow and develop are already in the workplace. Furthermore, climate at many colleges and universities is already supportive. There simply is no need for a separate organization and office called faculty development. In short, Toombs's argument is incorrect.

However, Toombs may be right about the managerial change that transpired as institutions grew and responded to a variety of forces. At the same time, he may be in error when he places the onus on the personnel policies of colleges and universities. However, rather than to pursue that line of inquiry, it seems more profitable to introduce some parameters that Toombs omitted for want of space.

One of these parameters is institutional type. There are appreciable differences in faculty life-styles across institutional strata. There are many faculty cultures, not just along discipline boundaries but also by type of institution. Consequently, personnel matters will be different for faculty at community colleges, small private liberal arts colleges, and large research universities. While personnel policies may be very similar at all three types right now, we can expect that major personnel revisions would not be identical in these different kinds of workplaces.

Another dimension that needs to be included is the differing requisites of the academic disciplines. For example, the age of major scholarly contribution is much younger in mathematics than it is in

English literature. For faculty who are going to be major producers of knowledge, the longer-term support that one field needs differs appreciably from the support needed for the other. The possibilities for alternative careers will not take place at the same time or in the same way for people in different disciplines. At the present time, however, sabbatical policies are the same for all disciplines.

Returning to Toombs's major thesis — that a major overhaul in personnel policies is needed — higher education could begin by reexamining its basic premises on employee expectations and by looking at career paths of other professionals in other kinds of organizations. What is needed is a healthy flow of people in and out of academe. Then, the surplus of existing and future talent could make its contributions as well as better permit the realization of human potential.

Some individuals will be single-career persons. As already noted, this path may be necessary for scholarship in some disciplines. But, we also know that about 10 percent of all academics produce 90 percent of all the research. Not everyone has to be a professor all her or his life in order to keep higher education vital. While we do not expect to see 90 percent of the faculty moving in and out of colleges and universities over their working lifetime, even an increase to as little as 25 percent — it is probably less than 1 percent now in chemistry, business, and a few professional fields — would have revolutionary organizational consequences.

One might learn from law school graduates or recipients of the bachelor's degree in architecture. Many of these individuals join firms and become the loyal working member that colleges and universities demand. However, a large number of these graduates have anything but the typical career. Lawyers can be found most everywhere today, including positions in higher education that are not in the legal domain at all. They move, and they change. Architects have just as checkered a career. Indeed, for both groups there are large numbers who never practice the profession for which they were formally schooled. Yet, they are failures neither to their profession nor to themselves.

Institutional loyalty is another bogeyman for colleges and universities. Administrators already criticize faculty for being more loyal to their discipline than they are to the organization. Professors are said not to care about the place at which they work. It is not our purpose here to disprove these falsehoods. Rather, we point out that the administrative value system that makes such statements is erroneous and needs changing. People can have multiple commitments and honor them all. No one ever thought that Adlai Stevenson was less loyal to the United States because he worked for a time for the United Nations and because he had a loyalty to its concerns for people of all nations.

In all, then, the issue of maintaining institutional vitality through the development of human resources—the faculty—confronts higher education with a new set of problems. This is not the first challenge to higher education in the faculty domain. It laid off academics during the Great Depression, and it graduated a lost generation not unlike that of today. It faced an acute shortage after World War II, it dealt with a modest oversupply in the early fifties, it made serious mistakes in the explosive sixties when it tenured low-quality people, and it went blindly into the 1970s as if expansion would never end. Perhaps it has learned something from its experiences in the past. Even if it has not, however, one can remain optimistic. After all, higher education feeds on solving problems.

References

Bowen, W. G. *Graduate Education in the Arts and Sciences: Prospects for the Future.* Princeton, N.J.: Princeton University, 1981.

Cartter, A. M. *Ph.D.s and the Academic Labor Market.* New York: McGraw-Hill, 1976.

Levinson, D. J., and others. *The Seasons of a Man's Life.* New York: Knopf, 1978.

McKeachie, W. J. "Faculty as a Renewable Resource." In R. Baldwin and R. Blackburn (Eds.), *College Faculty: Versatile Human Resources in a Period of Constraint.* New Directions for Institutional Research, no. 40. San Francisco: Jossey-Bass, 1983.

O'Connell, C. "The Influence of Organizational Policies and Arrangements of Faculty Development Programs upon Faculty Participation and Changed Classroom Behavior." Unpublished doctoral dissertation, University of Michigan, 1979.

Sarason, S. *Work, Aging, and Social Change: Professionals and the One Life—One Career Imperative.* New York: Free Press, 1977.

University of Chicago Record. *Report of the Commission on Graduate Education.* Chicago: University of Chicago, 1982, *16* (2), entire volume.

Robert T. Blackburn is professor of higher education in the Center for the Study of Higher Education at the University of Michigan.

Roger G. Baldwin is assistant to the provost at Wittenberg University.

Index

STATEMENT OF OWNERSHIP, MANAGEMENT, AND CIRCULATION
(Required by 39 U.S.C. 3685)

1. Title of Publication: New Directions for Institutional Research. A. Publication number: USPS 098-830. 2. Date of filing: September 30, 1983. 3. Frequency of issue: quarterly. A. Number of issues published annually: four. B. Annual subscription price: $35 institutions; $21 individuals. 4. Location of known office of publication: 433 California Street, San Francisco (San Francisco County), California 94104. 5. Location of the headquarters or general business offices of the publishers: 433 California Street, San Francisco (San Francisco County), California 94104. 6. Names and addresses of publisher, editor, and managing editor: publisher—Jossey-Bass Inc., Publishers, 433 California Street, San Francisco, California 94104; editor—Marvin Peterson, Center for Study of Higher Education, University of Michigan, Ann Arbor, MI 48109; managing editor—Allen Jossey-Bass, 433 California Street, San Francisco, California 94104. 7. Owner: Jossey-Bass Inc., Publishers, 433 California Street, San Francisco, California 94104. 8. Known bondholders, mortgages, and other security holders owning or holding 1 percent or more of total amount of bonds, mortgages, or other securities: same as No. 7. 10. Extent and nature of circulation: (Note: first number indicates the average number of copies of each issue during the preceding twelve months; the second number indicates the actual number of copies published nearest to filing date.) A. Total number of copies printed (net press run): 1990, 2012. B. Paid circulation, 1) Sales through dealers and carriers, street vendors, and counter sales: 85, 40. 2) Mail subscriptions: 963, 970. C. Total paid circulation: 1048, 1010. D. Free distribution by mail, carrier, or other means (samples, complimentary, and other free copies): 125, 125. E. Total distribution (sum of C and D): 1173, 1135. F. Copies not distributed, 1) Office use, left over, unaccounted, spoiled after printing: 817, 877. 2) Returns from news agents: 0, 0. G. Total (sum of E, F1, and 2—should equal net press run shown in A): 1990, 2012.

I certify that the statements made by me above are correct and complete.

JOHN R. WARD
Vice-President